HEBREW SYNTAX: AN OUTLINE

HEBREW SYNTAX
An Outline

RONALD J. WILLIAMS

UNIVERSITY OF TORONTO PRESS

Printed in Canada by
University of Toronto Press
Toronto and Buffalo

ISBN 0-8020-1451-8

To

THEOPHILE JAMES MEEK

(1881-1966)

אַשְׁרֵי אָדָם מָצָא חָכְמָה

וְאָדָם יָפִיק תְּבוּנָה

(Pr 3/13)

PREFACE

In offering this modest contribution to Hebrew studies, I am
acutely aware of my indebtedness to a host of scholars. The
brief bibliography at the end of this book is but a partial
indication of this debt. To all, especially those who gra-
ciously read the manuscript in its earlier stages, I would
express my obligation and gratitude.

The greatest debt of all, however, I owe to the late Professor T. J. Meek whose memory I revere as teacher, colleague
and friend. His profound understanding of the principles of
Hebrew syntax was the stimulation which aroused my special
interest in the subject, and which resulted in this volume.

For many years he taught a course in Hebrew syntax which
greatly enhanced Hebrew studies in the University of Toronto.
When this duty passed to me on his retirement, it was his in-
spiration and never-failing help that afforded me courage to
assume the task. We had hoped that during his retirement he
would provide us with the long-awaited fruits of his lifetime
studies. Ill health, alas, prevented this, and the present
work must serve as a poor substitute. That I have dedicated
it to him is a small token of my esteem and gratitude.

From the many students who have attended my classes all
through the years I have learned much. As one of the sages
observed long ago: הרבה למדתי מרבותי ומחברי יותר מרבותי
ומתלמידי יותר מכלם. To them all I offer my heartfelt thanks.

vii

For the generous loan of a Selectric Typewriter by the International Business Machines Corporation, and of a Hebrew typewriter by the Associated Hebrew Schools of Toronto, I am most grateful.

R. J. Williams

University of Toronto

April 20, 1967

ABBREVIATIONS

Am	Amos	Ju	Judges
Ca	Canticles	KAI	Donner-Röllig, _Kanaanäische_
Ch	Chronicles		_und Aramäische Inschriften_
Da	Daniel	Kg	Kings
Dt	Deuteronomy	La	Lamentations
Ec	Ecclesiastes	Lv	Leviticus
Es	Esther	Mi	Micah
Ex	Exodus	Na	Nahum
Ez	Ezra	Ne	Nehemiah
Ezk	Ezekiel	Nu	Numbers
Gn	Genesis	Ob	Obadiah
Ho	Hosea	Pr	Proverbs
Is	Isaiah	Ps	Psalms
Jb	Job	Ru	Ruth
Je	Jeremiah	Si	Sirach
Jl	Joel	Sm	Samuel
Jn	Jonah	UTB	Gordon, _Ugaritic Textbook_
Jo	Joshua	Zp	Zephaniah

HEBREW SYNTAX: AN OUTLINE

I. INTRODUCTION

While the morphology and lexicon of Hebrew are reasonably
well understood, its syntax has long been the most neglected
area of study. Many examples could be cited from the Revised
Standard Version to show that it is weak precisely at this
point. Likewise, although many of the emendations proposed
in the notes to Kittel's Biblia Hebraica reveal great ingenu-
ity on the part of the editors, they all too frequently dis-
play a shocking ignorance of the principles of Hebrew syntax.

Syntax, the relationship of words to one another, forms
together with morphology the material of grammar. Its relative importance varies according to the language considered.
This is particularly true in the case of word order, and may
be illustrated by languages as structurally different as
Sanskrit and Chinese. The former, a highly inflected language, allows great freedom in the order of words, since case
endings make the functions of words abundantly clear. On the
other hand, Chinese has no inflections, and consequently word
order assumes a prime importance and becomes inflexible; position is the key to the understanding of a Chinese sentence.
When an inflected language loses its case endings, as English
did, then word order and the increased use of prepositions
assume the functions of the former cases. That is why the
two statements the man hit the boy and the boy hit the man
have diametrically opposite meanings. Hebrew is in a similar

position to English, having early lost its case endings, and so depending largely on position for grammatical function. It is unfortunate that the significance of word order in Hebrew has not been fully appreciated by grammarians.

The contents of this volume have been developed over the past fifteen years as a series of notes dictated to classes in a formal course on Hebrew syntax at the University of Toronto. This has determined both their form and their brevity. The work makes no claim to be an exhaustive study but, as the title implies, merely an outline for the use of advanced classes in Hebrew.

Linguists may be dismayed by the fact that descriptions of syntactic functions offered are not exclusively intrinsic. That is to say, distinctions have sometimes been made by a comparison of the 'source language' (Hebrew) with the 'target language' (English). It is axiomatic that ideally only distinctions felt by native speakers of a language are valid. Nevertheless, years spent in teaching Hebrew to English-speaking students have shown the necessity of contrasting Hebrew usage with that of English. For this reason some further distinctions are desirable. There is, of course, no suggestion that the Hebrew speaker was conscious of the minute distinctions we have made. For instance, when making an utterance which required the use of the preposition ל he most certainly would not ask himself which of the nineteen uses of this preposition was being employed! For the learner of Hebrew, however, a careful cataloguing of the various nuances of such a morpheme is of real value for a full appreciation of

4

the range of meanings which it possesses.

This description is based on classical Hebrew prose, but some account is also taken of the deviations in later prose as well as in poetry. An important feature of the work is a selection of illustrative examples which should be carefully studied. All the quotations have been taken from the third edition of Kittel's Biblia Hebraica. A complete listing of the passages cited will be found at the end. A selected index of Hebrew words will make it possible for the reader to find the main discussions of particles not listed in the Table of Contents. Fairly exhaustive cross-references will then direct him to other sections dealing with them. The references in the text and the indexes are to the numbers of paragraphs.

The final chapter treats of the syntax of clauses. In some cases readers may feel that the term 'sentence' would be more appropriate. The fact is that, although the features of juncture in Hebrew make the recognition of clauses an easy task, the problem of defining the limits of a Hebrew sentence is difficult, and it is probably best to avoid the term.

Perhaps a word should be added concerning nomenclature. For the widely accepted terms 'absolute' and 'construct' I have adopted the more accurate linguistic expressions 'free form' and 'bound form,' the construction known as סְמִיכָה being designated as 'bound structure,' following a suggestion of my colleague Professor J. W. Wevers. To describe the בִּנְיָנִים of the verb, I have preferred the designation 'theme' to the less accurate 'stem' which has a much wider connotation. Since classical Hebrew had early abandoned the tense

5

concept in favour of an aspectual one, the use of 'aspect' in
place of 'tense' is desirable. To describe the verbal form
contained in the construction usually known as the 'waw-con-
secutive with the imperfect,' the word 'preterite' has been
chosen to indicate its original tense signification as well
as the fact that its origin was different from that of the
imperfect, as is shown by the weak verbs and the Hip‘îl of
strong verbs. 'Precative' has been employed for the indepen-
dent verbal form commonly designated 'jussive' or 'cohortative.' The latter expressions are restricted to certain persons of the verb, and a general term denoting the paradigm
as a whole is preferable. Finally, a word to describe verbal
roots other than stative is needed. Those in current use are
either 'active' (properly to be contrasted with 'passive') or
'intransitive' (the opposite of 'transitive'; yet many statives have direct objects). The more appropriate designation
'fientive' has been adopted.

II. SYNTAX OF THE NOUN

1. Number

(a) Singular

1 (i) To indicate a single person or thing, e.g. מִזְבֵּחַ, מֶלֶךְ.

2 (ii) To indicate a collective, e.g. עַם, בָּקָר, צֹאן; note
   that עֵץ, 'tree,' 'trees,' may be either a singular or a
   collective.

(b) Dual

3   Confined to substantives, since adjectives and verbs are
   inflected for singular and plural only.

4 (i) To indicate objects occurring naturally in pairs, e.g.
   יָדַיִם, אָזְנַיִם, נַעֲלַיִם (but always זְרֹעִים or זְרֹעוֹת!), even
   when more than two are mentioned, e.g. שֵׁשׁ כְּנָפַיִם (Is 6/2),
   אַרְבַּע רַגְלַיִם (Lv 11/23).

5 (ii) To indicate two of a kind, e.g. אַמָּתַיִם, שְׁנָתַיִם, יוֹמַיִם.

(c) Plural

6 (i) To indicate simple plurality, e.g. מְלָכִים, מִזְבְּחוֹת.

7 (ii) To indicate abstract ideas, e.g. זְקֻנִים, בְּתוּלִים,
   סְנְוֻרִים, חַיִּים, נְעוּרִים.

8 (iii) To indicate respect, often with attributive adjectives in the singular, e.g. אֱלֹהִים חַי (II Kg 19/4; but
   contrast אֱלֹהִים חַיִּים in I Sm 17/26), אֲדֹנִים קָשֶׁה (Is 19/4),
   קְבְרֹתֶיךָ (II Kg 22/20).

7

9 (iv) To indicate composition, e.g. עֲפָרוֹת, 'lumps,' 'earth
    clods' (Pr 8/26, Jb 28/6), עֵצִים, 'timber,' 'firewood'
    (but note Is 7/2, Ps 96/12), כְּסָפִים, 'silver pieces' (Gn
    42/25, 35).

10 (v) To indicate natural products in an unnatural condi-
    tion, e.g. חִטִּים, 'wheat' in grains (cf. חִטָּה in the ear),
    כֻּסְּמִים, 'spelt' (cf. כֻּסֶּמֶת), שְׂעֹרִים, 'barley' (cf. שְׂעֹרָה),
    דָּמִים, 'shed blood.'

11 (vi) Plural of extension, when the object consists of
    many parts, e.g. שָׁמַיִם, צַוָּארִים, פָּנִים.

  (d) Formation of Compound Plurals

12 (i) By pluralization of the first element, e.g. גִּבּוֹרֵי חַיִל
    (I Ch 7/2), בְּנֵי יְמִינִי (I Sm 22/7).

13 (ii) By pluralization of both elements, e.g. גִּבּוֹרֵי חֲיָלִים
    (I Ch 7/5), שָׂרֵי הַחֲיָלִים (I Kg 15/20), בָּתֵּי כְלָאִים (Is
    42/22).

14 (iii) By pluralization of the second element only, e.g.
    עִיר (I Kg 12/31), בֵּית בָּמוֹת (II Ch 25/5), בֵּית אָבוֹת
    מִבְצָרוֹת (Da 11/15).

  (e) Repetition

15 (i) Distributive (cf. § 100), e.g. יוֹם יוֹם (Gn 39/10),
    אִישׁ אִישׁ (Lv 17/10), יוֹם לַשָּׁנָה יוֹם לַשָּׁנָה, 'one day for
    each year' (Nu 14/34).

16 (ii) Emphasis, e.g. אֲשֶׁר זָהָב וַאֲשֶׁר־כֶּסֶף כָּסֶף, 'which were
    of pure gold and silver' (II Kg 25/15), גֵּבִים גֵּבִים, 'no-
    thing but trenches' (II Kg 3/16), מְעַט מְעַט, 'very gradu-
    ally' (Ex 23/30), שָׁלוֹם שָׁלוֹם, 'perfect peace' (Is 26/3);

8

cf. Gn 14/10, Nu 3/9, Dt 16/20.

2. Gender

(a) Masculine

17 (i) To indicate the male sex, e.g. אָב, מֶלֶךְ.

18 (ii) To indicate grammatical gender for inanimate objects,

e.g. בַּיִת, דָּבָר, לֵבָב.

19 (iii) In the plural to express abstract ideas (cf. § 7),

e.g. זְקֻנִים, חַיִּים.

(b) Feminine

20 (i) To indicate the female sex, e.g. אֵם, מַלְכָּה.

21 (ii) To indicate grammatical gender for inanimate objects,

e.g. אֵשׁ, כּוֹס, חֶרֶב.

22 (iii) Often to indicate parts of the body, especially

those occurring in pairs, e.g. קֶרֶן, אֹזֶן, רֶגֶל.

23 (iv) Proper names of countries and cities are usually con-

strued as feminine, e.g. מִצְרַיִם (Gn 41/8), מוֹאָב (II Sm

8/2), צֹר (Ezk 26/2).

24 (v) To express abstract ideas, e.g. אֱמוּנָה, 'faithful-

ness,' אַהֲבָה, 'love,' גְּבוּרָה, 'strength,' טוֹבָה, 'wel-

fare.' 'benefit.'

25 (vi) To express neuter concepts, e.g. זֹאת (II Kg 3/18),

וְנִפְלָאֹת, 'wonderful things' (Ex 34/10).

26 (vii) To form collectives, e.g. יוֹשֶׁבֶת, 'inhabitants,'

אֹיֶבֶת, 'enemies,' אֹרְחָה, 'caravan.'

27 (viii) To indicate the single component of a collective,

e.g. אֳנִיָּה, 'ship' (cf. אֳנִי, 'fleet'), שַׂעֲרָה, 'a hair' (cf. שֵׂעָר, 'hair').

3. Bound Structure (סְמִיכוּת)

28 Nouns may be combined into a single accentual unit in
which the second element delimits the range of the first,
e.g. דִּבְרֵי הַנְּבִיאִים (I Kg 22/13). The phonetic structure of
the language normally results in reduction of vowels in the
first component, which is a bound form. The second element,
a free form, is in the genitive relationship (cf. § 31), so
that the construction is quite comparable to that in modern
Welsh geiriau y proffwydi, 'the prophets' words,' where the
original case endings have also fallen away.

29 The bound form should be anarthrous (but note Phoenician
הברך בעל, 'blessed of Baal' (KAI, 26A 1/1) and Hebrew in
Ju 8/11, Jo 3/14, I Kg 14/24, II Kg 23/17 [twice], 25/19,
Je 25/26!), and directly precede its genitive, except when
two genitives are closely related, e.g. אֵם יַעֲקֹב וְעֵשָׂו (Gn
28/5); cf. Dt 10/18, Gn 14/19. Only one bound form may
precede the same genitive (but note the late expressions
סֵפֶר וּלְשׁוֹן כַּשְׂדִּים (Da 1/4) and מִבְחַר וְטוֹב-לְבָנוֹן (Ezk 31/16)).

30 However, the Directive הָ֫ may intervene in a bound structure (cf. § 62). Occasionally a bound form occurs before
prepositions, e.g. מַשְׁכִּימֵי בַבֹּקֶר (Is 5/11); cf. I Sm 9/3,
I Kg 22/13, II Sm 1/21, Ju 5/10. Rarely the bound form of
a substantive is followed by an adjective (cf. § 42), e.g.
כְּלֵי הַקָּטָן (Is 22/24); cf. Is 28/4, 16. The second element
of a bound structure may also be a noun clause (cf. § 489),

10

e.g. אָתָּם הִתְהַלַּכְנוּ פָּל־יְמֵי (I Sm 25/15). Some curious instances of hypallage should be noted, e.g. פָּל־עוֹד נַפְשִׁי בִּי
(II Sm 1/9);   cf. Jb 27/3, Is 19/8, Ho 14/3.

4. Case

31 The short vowels of the original case endings, preserved
in Ugaritic, Akkadian and classical Arabic, were lost in
Hebrew <u>ca</u>. 1000 B.C. It is thus strictly speaking incor-
rect to speak of cases in Hebrew. However, the names of
the three cases may be conveniently employed to designate
those syntactic functions of nouns which would be marked by
the appropriate case endings in an earlier period. That
classical Hebrew was still conscious of these separate
functions is clear from the use of the particle אֵת before
nouns in all situations which would require an accusative
case ending (cf. § 475).

 (a) <u>Nominative</u>
32 (i) Subject of a sentence, e.g. הַנָּחָשׁ הִשִּׁיאַנִי (Gn 3/13 and
     <u>passim</u>).
33 (ii) Predicative noun, which is regularly anarthrous,
     e.g. כִּי־גֵרִים הֱיִיתֶם בְּאֶרֶץ מִצְרָיִם (Dt 10/19); cf. Jo 2/17.
     When the article is present it expresses the superla-
     tive (cf. § 93), e.g. כִּי אַתֶּם הָרַבִּים (I Kg 18/25); cf.
     I Sm 9/21; or is the distinctive use of the article
     (cf. § 88), e.g. הַצַּדִּיק וַאֲנִי וְעַמִּי הָרְשָׁעִים ' (Ex 9/27).
34 (iii) Vocative, regularly with the article (cf. § 89),
     e.g. וַתֹּאמֶר הוֹשִׁעָה הַמֶּלֶךְ (II Sm 14/4).

11

35   (iv) Rhetorical absolute (casus pendens), a hanging nom-
      inative case resumed by a later word (cf. § 572), e.g.
      הַמָּקוֹם (Dt 12/11), הָאָרֶץ (Dt 11/10).

   (b) Genitive

36   This designates the grammatical function which occurs
      after bound forms, including prepositions.

37   (i) Subjective, e.g. דְּבַר-י׳ (Je 1/2), חָכְמַת שְׁלֹמֹה (I Kg
      5/10), אַהֲבַת י׳ (I Kg 10/9).

38   (ii) Objective, e.g. אֶרֶץ זָבַת חָלָב וּדְבָשׁ (Dt 6/3), חֲמַס אָחִיךָ,
      'the violence done to your brother' (Ob 10).

39   (iii) Possessive, e.g. בֵּית הַמֶּלֶךְ (I Kg 9/10), הֵיכַל י׳ (Je
      7/4).

40   (iv) Material, e.g. כְּלֵי כֶסֶף (I Kg 10/25), אֲרוֹן עֵץ (Dt
      10/1); so with numerals (cf. § 95), e.g. שְׁלֹשֶׁת יָמִים
      (Gn 30/36).

41   (v) Attributive, where English would employ an adjective,
      e.g. גִּבּוֹר חַיִל (I Sm 9/1), מֹאזְנֵי צֶדֶק (Lv 19/36), הַר-קָדְשִׁי
      (Ps 2/6).

42   (vi) Appositional, e.g. אֶרֶץ מִצְרַיִם (Ex 7/19), נְהַר-פְּרָת (Gn
      15/18), בַּת צִיּוֹן, 'the daughter Zion' (II Kg 19/21), אֵשֶׁת
      בַּעֲלַת-אוֹב (I Sm 28/7); cf. Ju 19/22. Also with adjec-
      tives, e.g. בִּשְׁנַת הַתְּשִׁיעִית (II Kg 17/6), עֹלַת הַתָּמִיד (Nu
      28/31).

43   (vii) Explicative, e.g. עֲצֵי שִׁטִּים, 'acacia wood' (Ex
      37/10), זֹבְחֵי אָדָם, 'men who sacrifice' (Ho 13/2).

44   (viii) Result, e.g. צֹאן טִבְחָה, 'sheep for the slaughter'
      (Ps 44/23, with which contrast צֹאן לְטִבְחָה in Je 12/3),

מוּסַר שְׁלוֹמֵנוּ, 'chastisement for our welfare' (Is 53/5).

45 (ix) Agent or means, after the bound form of a passive participle, e.g. מֻכֵּה אֱלֹהִים, 'smitten by God' (Is 53/4), שְׂרֻפוֹת אֵשׁ, 'burned with fire' (Is 1/7).

46 (x) Specification or epexegetical, after the bound form of an adjective, e.g. קְשֵׁה־עֹרֶף (Ex 32/9), יְפֵה־תֹאַר (Gn 39/6).

47 (xi) Superlative, e.g. שִׁיר הַשִּׁירִים (Ca 1/1), אֱלֹהֵי הָאֱלֹהִים (Dt 10/17); cf. Ex 29/37.

48 (xii) Measure or number (rare), e.g. מְתֵי מִסְפָּר, 'a few men' (Gn 34/30), מֵי מָתְנָיִם, 'water up to the thighs' (Ezk 47/4); contrast § 69.

49 (xiii) Dependent, after prepositions: passim.

(c) Accusative

50 (i) Direct object of a verb, e.g. וַיִּבְרָא אֱלֹהִים אֶת־הָאָדָם (Gn 1/27 and passim).

51 (ii) Cognate accusative, e.g. פָּחֲדוּ פָחַד (Ps 14/5), חָטָא חָטְאָה יְרוּשָׁלַ͏ִם (La 1/8); cf. II Kg 4/13, 13/14.

52 (iii) Product or result, e.g. וַיִּבְנֶה אֶת־הָאֲבָנִים מִזְבֵּחַ (I Kg 18/32); cf. I Sm 8/1.

53 (iv) Material, e.g. וַיִּיצֶר יְ' אֱלֹהִים אֶת־הָאָדָם עָפָר (Gn 2/7), וַיִּרְגְּמוּ אֹתוֹ כָל־יִשְׂרָאֵל אֶבֶן (Jo 7/25); cf. Dt 27/6.

54 (v) Directive or terminative, after verbs of motion, e.g. וְצֵא הַשָּׂדֶה, 'go out to the field' (Gn 27/3). The apparent exceptions בֵּית (e.g. II Kg 19/37) and פֶּתַח (e.g. II Kg 5/9) are really bound forms of substantives used loca- tively as prepositions (probably in the accusative of

13

manner, cf. § 60), similarly to דֶּרֶךְ, 'towards,' מוּל, 'opposite,' אֵצֶל, 'beside' (Dt 11/30).

55 (vi) Separative, only after יָצָא, e.g. בָּנַי יְצָאֻנִי וְאֵינָם(Je 10/20); cf. Gn 44/4, Am 4/3.

56 (vii) Temporal, expressing duration of time, e.g. כָּל־יְמֵי חַיֶּיךָ (Gn 3/14); cf. Ex 13/7 (N.B. אֵת), Dt 9/25. Contrast II Sm 2/10 with Gn 47/18, הַלַּיְלָה with בַּבֹּקֶר (Ru 3/13), Jo 8/3 with Gn 26/24, הַיּוֹם with בַּיּוֹם.

57 (viii) Specification, e.g. חָלָה אֶת־רַגְלָיו (I Kg 15/23), לֹא נַכֶּנּוּ נָפֶשׁ (Gn 37/21); cf. Gn 41/40, II Sm 15/32. This may sometimes be a clause (cf. § 492). Here belongs the predicative accusative (contrast the predicative nominative, § 33) which is anarthrous, e.g. וַיִּשְׁמַע מֹשֶׁה אֶת־הָעָם בֹּכֶה (Nu 11/10), אֹתְךָ רָאִיתִי צַדִּיק (Gn 7/1); cf. I Sm 9/11.

58 (ix) Emphatic accusative of specification, when the accusative is the semantic subject which precedes the verb, with concord of person, number and gender, e.g. יָדַעְתָּ וַיִּרְאוּ הַמִּצְרִים (II Sm 3/25), אֶת־אַבְנֵר בֶּן־נֵר כִּי לְפַתֹּתְךָ בָּא אֶת־הָאִשָּׁה כִּי־יָפָה הִוא מְאֹד (Gn 12/14); cf. I Kg 5/17, Gn 1/4. Occasionally no verb precedes, e.g. וְאֶת־הַבַּרְזֶל נָפַל אֶל־הַמָּיִם (II Kg 6/5); cf. Nu 11/22 (here the following verb is singular!), Ju 6/28, II Sm 21/22. In place of a finite verb, it may be followed by a construct infinitive, e.g. וַיִּשְׁאַל אֶת־נַפְשׁוֹ לָמוּת (I Kg 19/4); contrast I Kg 19/10. This differs only slightly from the rhetorical absolute (cf. § 35); note the example וְאִישׁ אֶת־קָדָשָׁיו לוֹ יִהְיוּ, 'as for anyone, in the matter of his

14

sacred things, they shall be his' (Nu 5/10), where אִישׁ
is a rhetorical absolute and אֶת־קָ׳ an emphatic accusative of specification.

59   (x) Determinative, in which the apparent object is really
the subject, and follows the verb without concord, since
it is impersonal and often passive, e.g. וַיֻּגַּד לְרִבְקָה אֶת־
דִּבְרֵי עֵשָׂו (Gn 27/42); cf. Gn 17/5, Am 4/2, Dt 12/22,
I Kg 2/21, II Sm 11/25, Ne 9/32, I Sm 20/13, and note
medieval Latin legitur Vergilium. This may also occur
with an infinitive, e.g. בְּהִוָּלֶד לוֹ אֵת אֶת יִצְחָק בְּנוֹ (Gn 21/5);
cf. Gn 21/8, Nu 7/10, or with a clause (cf. § 493),
e.g. הֻגַּד הֻגַּד לַעֲבָדֶיךָ אֵת אֲשֶׁר צִוָּה יְ׳ וְג׳ (Jo 9/24). Exceptions, in which the verb exhibits concord, are Nu 17/2
f., II Kg 18/30 (= Is 36/15) and Gn 29/27. In הַמְעַט־
לָנוּ אֶת־עֲוֹן פְּעוֹר (Jo 22/17) the predicate is not a verb,
but an adjective.

60   (xi) Manner is expressed by the accusative, which is also
known as the adverbial accusative. It is anarthrous,
e.g. וַתֵּשְׁבוּ בֶּטַח (I Sm 12/11), קוֹמְמִיּוּת, 'erect' (Lv 26/13);
cf. I Sm 13/17; so also in the case of מְאֹד, הַרְבֵּה, etc.
This may even, on occasion, be a clause (cf. § 491).

5. Directive הָ֫

61 That this is not the old accusative ending is shown by
the evidence of Ugaritic, in which arṣh = אַ֫רְצָה, šmmh =
הַשָּׁמַ֫יְמָה. Note that this ending is not present in שָׁמָּה,
Ugaritic tmt, where the ending is an original deictic t

15

as in Ugaritic <u>hmt</u> = הֵ֫מָּה; cf. II Kg 23/8.

62 (a) Directive or terminative, e.g. הַבֶּט־נָא הַשָּׁמַ֫יְמָה (Gn
    15/5), הָבֵא אֶת־הָאֲנָשִׁים הַבָּ֫יְתָה (Gn 43/16). This ending may
    intervene between a bound form and its genitive (cf.
    § 30), e.g. בֵּ֫יתָה יוֹסֵף (Gn 43/17), מִדְבַּ֫רָה דַמֶּ֫שֶׂק (I Kg
    19/15).

63 (b) Temporal, meaning 'until,' e.g. מִיָּמִים יָמִ֫ימָה, 'from
    year to year' (Ex 13/10, Ju 11/40).

64 (c) Occasionally separative, e.g. מִבָּבֶ֫לָה (Je 27/16),
    מִצָּפ֫וֹנָה (Jo 15/10). Note the irregular use with בְּ,
    e.g. I Sm 23/15, 18 f., 31/13, II Sm 20/15, or אֵ֫צֶל,
    e.g. I Kg 4/12 (all proper names!).

6. Apposition

65 (a) Genus and species, e.g. אִשָּׁה אַלְמָנָה (I Kg 7/14), נַעֲרָה
    בְתוּלָה (I Kg 1/2), אִישׁ כֹּהֵן (Lv 21/9).

66 (b) Attributive, where the second element is equivalent
    to an adjective (contrast § 41), e.g. אֲמָרִים אֱמֶת, 'true
    words' (Pr 22/21), יַ֫יִן תַּרְעֵלָה, 'intoxicating wine,' lit.
    'wine, staggering' (Ps 60/5), לָשׁוֹן רְמִיָּה (Ps 120/3).

67 (c) Predicative, when a substantive is used in place of
    an adjective, e.g. אֱמֶת הָיָה הַדָּבָר (I Kg 10/6), הֲשָׁלוֹם
    אֲבִיכֶם הַזָּקֵן (Gn 43/27).

68 (d) Material, e.g. הַבָּקָר הַנְּחֹ֫שֶׁה (II Kg 16/17); cf. I Ch
    15/19; סְאָה־סֹ֫לֶת (II Kg 7/1), שְׁנָתַ֫יִם יָמִים (Gn 41/1); cf.
    II Kg 3/4, 5/17, Ex 39/17. So with numerals, e.g. שְׁלֹשָׁה
    בָנִים (contrast § 40). Occasionally the first element

16

has the article while the second is anarthrous, e.g.
הַמַּבּוּל מַיִם (Gn 6/17); cf. Phoenician זן נחשת המזבח
(KAI, 10/4).

69 (e) Measure or number, e.g. יָמִים מִסְפָּר (Nu 9/20), מַיִם
    בִּרְכַּיִם, 'water extending to the knees' (Ezk 47/4);
    contrast § 48.

70 (f) Explicative, giving the name or title, e.g. הָאָרֶץ
    כְּנַעַן (Nu 34/2), לִשְׁלֹמֹה הַמֶּלֶךְ (I Kg 2/17), the former
    being the commoner order (contrast § 42). When the
    name follows, any preposition or the accusative par-
    ticle is repeated, e.g. Gn 24/4, 4/2 (but note the
    exceptions in Gn 24/12, I Sm 25/19, Jb 1/8), whereas
    when the name precedes this is not so, e.g. Gn 4/8,
    16/3.

71 (g) Anticipative, with pronominal suffixes. This is com-
    mon in Aramaic and Ethiopic, but rare in Hebrew, e.g.
    וַתִּרְאֵהוּ אֶת־הַיֶּלֶד (Ex 2/6), בְּבֹאוֹ הָאִישׁ (Ezk 10/3); cf.
    I Kg 21/13.

7. Hendiadys

72 A single concept may be expressed by two words linked
    with the conjunction וְ, e.g. חָמָס וָשֹׁד (Am 3/10, Je 6/7,
    20/8, Ezk 45/9), cf. English 'assault and battery'; נִין
    וָנֶכֶד (Is 14/22, Gn 21/23, Jb 18/19), cf. 'kith and kin';
    חֶסֶד וֶאֱמֶת, 'true loyalty' (Ex 34/6, Jo 2/14, II Sm 2/6,
    15/20; in Pr 16/6 only one preposition is used!); הַבְּרִית
    וְהַחֶסֶד, 'loving faith' (Dt 7/9, 12, I Kg 8/23, Ne 9/32);

17

הֹוד וְהָדָר, 'glorious splendour' (Jb 40/10); חֹשֶׁךְ וְצַלְמָוֶת,
'blackest darkness' (Jb 10/21); דְּמָמָה וָקֹול (Jb 4/16);
תֹּהוּ וָבֹהוּ (Gn 1/2).

8. Adjectives

73   (a) Attributive adjectives follow their substantives,
with concord of gender, number and determination, e.g.
אֱלֹהִים אֲחֵרִים (Dt 8/19), בִּתִּי הַגְּדֹולָה (I Sm 18/17). With
dual substantives the plural is used, e.g. יָדַיִם רָפֹות
and בִּרְכַּיִם כֹּרְעֹות (Jb 4/3 f.), and this may also occur
with collectives, e.g. הָעָם הַנִּמְצָאִים (I Sm 13/15); cf.
Gn 30/36. Plurals of respect may be followed by the
singular or the plural (cf. § 8). Attributive adjectives follow all the constituent elements of a bound
structure, exhibiting concord with the component to
which they refer, e.g. בִּגְדֵי עֵשָׂו בְּנָהּ הַגָּדֹל הַחֲמֻדֹת (Gn
27/15). Anomalous instances of an anarthrous substantive with a determinated adjective do occur, e.g. חָצֵר
הַגְּדֹולָה (I Kg 7/12); cf. Ezk 40/28, Je 6/20, I Sm 12/23.

74   (b) Demonstrative adjectives follow their substantives
and any attributive adjectives (but note Je 13/10, II
Ch 1/10), with concord of gender, number and determin-
ation, e.g. הַמִּשְׁפָּחָה הָרָעָה הַזֹּאת (Je 8/3), בַּיָּמִים הָרַבִּים הָהֵם
(Ex 2/23); but note בַּלַּיְלָה הוּא in Gn 19/33, 30/16,
32/23, I Sm 19/10. However, they do not take the article when modifying a substantive determinated only by
reason of a pronominal suffix, but are used in apposi-

tion, e.g. לֵךְ בְּכֹחֲךָ זֶה (Ju 6/14); cf. Dt 5/29, Jo 2/20, II Kg 1/13, Gn 24/8; but note Jo 2/17 and II Ch 1/10!

75 (c) Predicative adjectives may precede or follow their substantives, with concord of gender and number, but are normally anarthrous (cf. §§ 33, 57), e.g. וְהֶעָרִים רַבִּים (Gn 6/5), רַבָּה רָעַת הָאָדָם (Nu 13/28), בְּצֻרֹת גְּדֹלֹת מְאֹד רַחֲמָיו (I Ch 21/13). However, when they precede, they need not exhibit concord, e.g. יָשָׁר מִשְׁפָּטֶיךָ (Ps 119/137).

76 (d) Comparison is expressed by מִן (cf. §§ 317 f.), e.g. כִּי־הָיָה רְכוּשָׁם רָב מִשֶּׁבֶת יַחְדָּו (I Sm 9/2), גָּבֹהַּ מִכָּל־הָעָם 'their possessions were too great for them to live together' (Gn 36/7); cf. I Kg 8/64.

(e) The superlative is expressed:

77 (i) By a determinated adjective, e.g. בְּנוֹ הַקָּטָן, 'his youngest son' (Gn 9/24); cf. § 93.

78 (ii) By a bound structure, e.g. קְטֹן בָּנָיו, 'the youngest of his sons' (II Ch 21/17).

79 (iii) By means of a pronominal suffix, e.g. טוֹבָם, 'the best of them' (Mi 7/4), מִגְּדוֹלָם וְעַד־קְטַנָּם (Jn 3/5).

80 (iv) By means of a superlative genitive (cf. § 47), e.g. עֶבֶד עֲבָדִים (Gn 9/25), הֲבֵל הֲבָלִים (Ec 1/2).

81 (v) By using a divine epithet, e.g. עִיר־גְּדוֹלָה לֵאלֹהִים (Jn 3/3), וַתְּהִי לְחֶרְדַּת אֱלֹהִים (I Sm 14/15); cf. Gn 35/5, I Sm 11/7, Ps 80/11, 36/7. So also in Ugaritic, e.g. <u>t</u>lḥn il, 'a gorgeous table' (<u>UTB</u>, 51.i.39).

9. Article

82 The article is regularly omitted from bound forms and

19

substantives with pronominal suffixes (but cf. § 29 and note the anomalous forms in Lv 27/23, Jo 7/21, 8/33, II Kg 15/16, Gn 31/13, Ex 9/18, II Kg 23/17, Is 36/16, Ezk 46/19, Ps 123/4). This does not, of course, apply to participles with the relative article (cf. § 90), e.g. הַמַּאֲכִלְךָ מָן (Dt 8/16); cf. Dt 20/1, Is 9/12, Ps 18/33, Ju 8/11. The article is rare in poetry which, being some-what archaic in its language, reflects the period before the development of the article, e.g. קֹנֵה שָׁמַיִם וָאָרֶץ (Gn 14/19).

83　(a) Definite, especially when the person or thing has al-ready been mentioned, e.g. וַיֹּאמֶר הַמֶּלֶךְ קְחוּ לִי־חֶרֶב וַיָּבִאוּ הַחֶרֶב לִפְנֵי הַמֶּלֶךְ (I Kg 3/24); cf. Gn 18/7 f.

84　(b) The article is employed when the object or person is definite in the thought of the narrator, although such words are indefinite in English, e.g. בַּסֵּפֶר (I Sm 10/25), וַיְהִי הַיּוֹם (II Kg 4/8); cf. I Sm 9/9, Jo 2/15.

85　(c) As in English, the article is used when an object or person is a well-known or recognized fact, e.g. וַיִּקַּח אַבְרָהָם אֶת־עֲצֵי הָעֹלָה . . . וַיִּקַּח בְּיָדוֹ אֶת־הָאֵשׁ וְאֶת־הַמַּאֲכֶלֶת (Gn 22/6); cf. II Sm 18/24.

86　(d) Possessive, e.g. וְלָקַח דָּוִד אֶת־הַכִּנּוֹר, 'David would take his lyre' (I Sm 16/23); cf. Gn 24/65.

87　(e) Demonstrative, e.g. הַיּוֹם, 'today' (I Sm 24/19), הַפַּעַם, 'this time' (Gn 2/23).

88　(f) Distinctive, e.g. הָאֱלֹהִים, 'the true God' (I Kg 18/39), הַנָּהָר, 'the Euphrates' (Gn 31/21).

89　(g) Vocative (cf. § 34), e.g. הוֹשִׁיעָה אֲדֹנִי הַמֶּלֶךְ (II Kg

6/26).

(h) Relative, i.e. equivalent to a relative pronoun:

90   (i) With a participle (cf. § 218), e.g. ‏/ הַנִּרְאֶה אֵלָיו‎
(Gn 12/7); cf. II Kg 22/18.

91   (ii) With a perfect aspect, e.g. ‏וְכֹל הַהִקְדִּישׁ שְׁמוּאֵל‎ (I Ch
26/28), ‏הֶהָלְכוּא אִתּוֹ‎ (Jo 10/24); cf. I Kg 11/9, Ez
8/25, 10/14, 17.

92 (i) Generic, to express classes, e.g. ‏הַכֶּלֶב‎ (Ju 7/5), ‏הָעֹרֵב‎
(Gn 8/7), ‏הַכְּנַעֲנִי‎ (Ju 1/1), ‏הַצַּדִּיק‎ (Ec 3/17). This is
the normal use in comparisons, e.g. ‏אֲדֻמִּים כַּדָּם‎ (II Kg
3/22); cf. II Kg 5/27, I Sm 9/9, 17/34, Am 5/19.

93 (j) Superlative (cf. § 77), e.g. ‏וּרְאִיתֶם הַטּוֹב וְהַיָּשָׁר מִבְּנֵי‎
‏אֲדֹנֵיכֶם‎ (II Kg 10/3); cf. Dt 7/7.

10. Numerals

(a) Cardinal

94 (i) 'One' is an attributive adjective (cf. § 73), e.g.
‏אִישׁ אֶחָד‎ (Ju 18/19),‏אִשָּׁה אַחַת‎ (II Kg 4/1), ‏הַמַּחֲנֶה הָאַחַת‎
(Gn 32/9). Sometimes ‏אֶחָד‎ is anarthrous, even when its
substantive is determinated, e.g. ‏הָרֹאשׁ אֶחָד‎ (I Sm
13/17 f.).

95 (ii) 'Two' to 'ten' are substantives which may precede
the numbered object in the bound structure, the object
being in the plural of the genitive of material (cf. §
40), or be in the free form with the object as an apposition of material (cf. § 68), in both cases without
concord of gender (except for 'two'), e.g. ‏חֲמֵשֶׁת מַלְכֵי‎

וְחָמֵשׁ מֵאוֹת (II Kg 25/19), וַחֲמִשָּׁה אֲנָשִׁים or (Nu 31/8) מִדְיָן
אֻמּוֹת later also ,(I Sm 25/42) וְחָמֵשׁ נַעֲרֹתֶיהָ or (Jb 1/3)
שְׁתֵּי נָשִׁים (II Sm 4/2), שְׁנֵי אֲנָשִׁים but ;(II Ch 3/11) חָמֵשׁ
shown (I Ch 4/5); cf. שִׁבְעָה בָנִים וְשָׁלוֹשׁ בָּנוֹת (Jb 1/2). For exceptions to the rule with regard to gender see Gn 7/13,
I Sm 10/3, Jb 1/4.

96   (iii) '11-19' and multiples of ten are substantives which
      normally precede in apposition to the object enumerated
      which is in the plural (except, after 11-19, for a few
      common words, viz. יוֹם, שָׁנָה, שֶׁקֶל, נֶפֶשׁ, אִישׁ), the digit
      showing inversion of gender, e.g. חֲמִשָּׁה עָשָׂר בָּנִים (II Sm
      9/10); cf. Jo 4/8. Multiples of ten, when preceding,
      take the enumerated object in the plural, e.g. אַרְבָּעִים
      בָּנִים (Ju 12/14), except for the common words אִישׁ, אֶלֶף,
      כֹּר, שֶׁקֶל, נֶפֶשׁ, שָׁנָה, יוֹם (cf. II Sm 15/1), but if the
      numbered object precedes, the plural is always used,
      e.g. כֶּסֶף־שְׁקָלִים אַרְבָּעִים (Ne 5/15). When the expression
      is definite the article may be prefixed either to the
      numeral, e.g. שְׁנֵים הֶעָשָׂר אִישׁ (Jo 4/4), or to the accom-
      panying substantive, e.g. שְׁתֵּים עֶשְׂרֵה הָאֲבָנִים הָאֵלֶּה (Jo
      4/20); cf. Ju 17/2, Gn 18/28.

97   (iv) Multiples of ten plus units take the enumerated ob-
      ject either after, in the singular, e.g. שְׁתַּיִם וְשִׁשִּׁים שָׁנָה
      (Gn 5/20), or before, in the plural, e.g. וְאַחֲרֵי הַשָּׁבֻעִים
      שִׁשִּׁים וּשְׁנַיִם (Da 9/26). Note also the construction חָמֵשׁ
      שָׁנִים וְשִׁבְעִים שָׁנָה (Gn 12/4). The article may be prefixed
      to the numerals, e.g. הַשְּׁלֹשָׁה וְהַשִּׁבְעִים וְהַמָּאתָיִם (Nu 3/46)
      or the accompanying substantive, e.g. Da 9/26 above.

22

(b) Ordinal

98 (i) 'First' to 'tenth' are attributive adjectives (cf.
§ 73), e.g. בַּשָּׁנָה הַשֵּׁנִית (Gn 47/18). Sometimes they occur
after the bound form of the thing numbered, e.g. יוֹם
הַשְּׁבִיעִי (Dt 5/14); cf. II Kg 17/6. This is the appositional genitive (cf. § 42). Rarely the bound form of
the substantive is followed by the cardinal numeral,
e.g. בִּשְׁנַת שְׁתַּיִם (II Kg 15/32); cf. II Kg 18/10. Occasionally the cardinal numeral is employed for 'first,'
e.g. שֵׁם הָאֶחָד . . . וְשֵׁם הַשֵּׁנִי (II Sm 4/2).

99 (ii) 'Eleventh,' etc. The cardinal numerals are employed,
e.g. בְּשִׁבְעָה־עָשָׂר יוֹם (Gn 7/11), בִּשְׁנַת עֶשְׂרִים וָשֶׁבַע (I Kg
16/10), the enumerated object being anarthrous. When
the expression is definite, the article may be attached
to the numeral, e.g. וְהוּא בִּשְׁנֵים הֶעָשָׂר (I Kg 19/19),
and exceptionally הַשְׁנֵים עָשָׂר (I Ch 25/19), although this
is not required, e.g. וַיְהִי בְּאַרְבָּעִים שָׁנָה בְּעַשְׁתֵּי־עָשָׂר חֹדֶשׁ
(Dt 1/3).

(c) Distributive

100 (i) Simple repetition (cf. § 15), e.g. שְׁנַיִם שְׁנַיִם, 'two by
two' (Gn 7/9, 15), בַּבֹּקֶר בַּבֹּקֶר (Ex 30/7).

101 (ii) Repetition with the conjunction וְ (cf. § 442), e.g.
דּוֹר־וָדוֹר (Dt 32/7), שֵׁשׁ וָשֵׁשׁ, 'six each' (II Sm 21/20).

102 (iii) Repetition with the preposition בְּ (cf. § 254), e.g.
חֶדֶר בְּחָדֶר (I Kg 20/30), שָׁנָה בְשָׁנָה (II Kg 17/4); cf. I
Sm 1/7, II Ch 30/21, I Ch 12/23.

103 (iv) By means of the preposition לְ (cf. § 281), e.g.

23

לְמֵאוֹת וְלַאֲלָפִים, 'by hundreds and thousands' (I Sm 29/2);
cf. Am 4/4.

104 (v) Sometimes a word (usually a participle) occurs in the
plural with a singular predicate expressing the meaning
'everyone who,' e.g. וְתֹמְכֶיהָ מְאֻשָּׁר (Pr 3/18), מְחַלְלֶיהָ מוֹת
יוּמָת (Ex 31/14); cf. Gn 27/29, Lv 17/14.

105 (vi) The substantive כֹּל followed by an indefinite substantive may have a distributive sense, e.g. סֻגַּר כָּל־
בַּיִת מִבּוֹא (Is 24/10); cf. Gn 2/9, Ru 4/7.

11. Pronouns

(a) Independent Personal

106 (i) As subject of a finite verb for emphasis or contrast,
e.g. וְאַתָּה תִּמְשָׁל־בּוֹ, 'you are the one who must master it'
(Gn 4/7); cf. Dt 5/31.

107 (ii) In apposition to a pronominal suffix (in genitive or
accusative functions), e.g. בָּרְכֵנִי גַם־אָנִי (Gn 27/34),
כִּי אִתָּנוּ אֲנַחְנוּ (Dt 5/3), מִי־יִתֵּן מוּתִי אֲנִי (II Sm 19/1);
cf. I Kg 21/19, II Sm 17/5. As a rhetorical absolute
(cf. § 35) in the following: גַּם אָנֹכִי חָלִילָה לִּי (I Sm
12/23).

108 (iii) As subject of a participle, e.g. אָנֹכִי מְצַוְּךָ הַיּוֹם
(Dt 8/1).

(b) Suffixed Personal

109 (i) Subjective, e.g. אָכָלְכֶם (Gn 3/5), בְּהִבָּרְאָם (Gn 2/4),
עָבְרִי (Dt 4/21).

110 (ii) Objective, e.g. וַיַּנִּחֵהוּ . . . לְעָבְדָהּ (Gn 2/15), חֲמָסִי,

24

'the wrong done to me' (Gn 16/5), לְדָרְשֵׁנִי (Je 37/7).

111 (iii) Possessive, e.g. בְּרִיתִי (Gn 6/18), מַלְכֵּנוּ (Ps 89/19).

112 (iv) After prepositions only the suffixed forms of pronouns are used.

(c) Demonstrative (Deictic)

113 זֶה is employed when something is first mentioned or
about to be mentioned; הוּא indicates something already
mentioned, e.g. וְהָיָה אֲשֶׁר אֹמַר אֵלֶיךָ זֶה יֵלֵךְ אִתָּךְ הוּא יֵלֵךְ
אִתָּךְ (Ju 7/4).

114 (i) Explicative, e.g. זֶה הַיּוֹם (Ju 4/14), אֵלֶּה שְׁמוֹת בְּנֵי־
עֵשָׂו (Gn 36/10).

115 (ii) Anaphoric, e.g. יְ הוּא הָאֱלֹהִים (I Kg 18/39), אֶרֶץ
מִצְרַיִם לְפָנֶיךָ הִוא (Gn 47/6). Note that this form is
used even with a first person, e.g. אֲנִי־הוּא הַמְדַבֵּר
(Is 52/6), or a second person, e.g. אַתָּה־הוּא הָאֱלֹהִים
(II Sm 7/28).

116 (iii) Antithetical, when repeated to express a contrast,
e.g. זֶה . . . זֶה, 'this . . . that,' 'the one . . .
the other' (Is 6/3), אֵלֶּה . . . אֵלֶּה, 'some . . .
others' (Jo 8/22).

117 (iv) Adjectival, either as an attributive adjective,
e.g. הַדְּבָרִים הָאֵלֶּה (I Sm 18/23), or in apposition, e.g.
זֹאת הָרָעָה (II Kg 6/33), אֵלֶּה הַצֹּאן (I Ch 21/17); cf.
§ 74.

118 (v) Enclitic, as an undeclined particle for emphasis,
e.g. מַה־זֶּה, 'what in the world?' (I Sm 10/11), לָמָּה־
זֶּה, 'why ever?' (I Sm 17/28), הִנֵּה־זֶה (I Kg 19/5),

25

עֹשֶׂה זֶה (I Kg 17/24), הַאַתָּה זֶה בְּנִי, 'Are you <u>really</u> my
son?' (Gn 27/21); cf. I Kg 18/7, 17, Nu 13/17. With
the verb עָשָׂה the form זֹאת is always used, e.g. מַה־זֹּאת
עָשִׂית (Gn 3/13); cf. Gn 42/28. The unchangeable form
זֶה regularly precedes in expressions such as זֶה עֶשְׂרִים
שָׁנָה, 'for twenty years now' (Gn 31/38); cf. Gn 27/36,
43/10.

(d) Interrogative

119   The forms מִי and מָה are indeclinable.

(i) מִי

120   (1) Interrogative, 'who?', e.g. מִי הִגִּיד לְךָ (Gn 3/11);
       cf. Ju 18/3.

121   (2) Indefinite, 'whoever,' e.g. מִי לַי/ אֵלָי (Ex 32/26);
       cf. Ju 7/3.

122   (3) Desiderative or optative, to be rendered 'would
       that!', 'if only!', as in מִי־יְשִׂמֵנִי שֹׁפֵט בָּאָרֶץ (II Sm
       15/4). It is usually expanded to מִי־יִתֵּן (cf. § 546).

123   (4) Adverbial, 'how?', is rare, e.g. מִי יָקוּם יַעֲקֹב (Am
       7/2, 5).

(ii) מָה

124   (1) Interrogative, 'what?', e.g. מֶה עָשִׂיתָ (Gn 4/10);
       cf. Gn 37/26.

125   (2) Adverbial, 'how?', e.g. מָה אֶתֵּן זֶה לִפְנֵי מֵאָה אִישׁ (II
       Kg 4/43); cf. Gn 44/16, Nu 23/8; or 'why?', e.g.
       מָה־אוֹחִיל לַי/ עוֹד (II Kg 6/33); cf. II Kg 7/3, Ex
       14/15, although this is usually לָמָּה.

126   (3) Indefinite, 'whatever,' is rare, e.g. וּדְבַר מַה־

יַרְאֵנִי וְהִגַּדְתִּי לָךְ (Nu 23/3); cf. I Sm 19/3.

127   (4) Exclamatory, 'how!', e.g. מַה־נּוֹרָא הַמָּקוֹם הַזֶּה (Gn
28/17); cf. Nu 24/5.

128   (5) Negative (cf. § 428), a rare use arising from its
employment in rhetorical questions, e.g. מַה־לָּנוּ חֵלֶק
בְּדָוִד וְלֹא־נַחֲלָה בְּבֶן־יִשַׁי (I Kg 12/16; parallel to
אֵין in II Sm 20/1); cf. Ca 8/4 (note the parallel
with privative אִם in 2/7).

(e) Relative

129   The true relative pronoun זִי, found in Phoenician,
e.g. בת ז בני יחמלך (KAI, 4/1), is preserved in Hebrew
only as an archaism in poetry, e.g. עַם־זוּ גָּאָלְתָּ (Ex
15/13); cf. Ex 15/16, Ps 9/16, 10/2; וְעֵדֹתִי זוֹ אֲלַמְּדֵם,
'my statutes which I will teach them' (Ps 132/12),
לִוְיָתָן זֶה־יָצַרְתָּ (Ps 104/26); cf. Jb 19/19. In north
Palestinian and late Hebrew the form שֶׁ is also found
(Ju 7/12, II Kg 6/11, Ec 1/14; cf. §§ 470 f.). Otherwise the relative is expressed by the particle אֲשֶׁר (cf.
§§ 462 f.) as in Moabite.

(f) Reflexive

130   Hebrew has no partitive, distributive, reciprocal or
reflexive pronouns. The last may be expressed by the
use of suffixed personal pronouns, e.g. הַאֹתִי הֵם מַכְעִסִים
הֲלוֹא אֹתָם . . ., 'Do they anger me? Is it not themselves?' (Je 7/19), or by נֶפֶשׁ. That these are inter-
changeable is clear from a comparison of נִשְׁבַּע אֲדֹנָי יְ'
בְּנַפְשׁוֹ (Am 6/8) with אֲשֶׁר נִשְׁבַּעְתָּ לָהֶם בָּךְ (Ex 32/13). The

27

reflexive idea may also be expressed by the N<u>ip</u>ʿal or
H<u>itp</u>ō̄ʿel themes   (cf. §§ 135, 152, 154 f.).

(g) <u>Distributive</u>

131   To express the distributive 'each' Hebrew employs אִישׁ,
e.g. וַיַּחַלְמוּ חֲלוֹם שְׁנֵיהֶם אִישׁ חֲלֹמוֹ (Gn 40/5);   cf. Ex
12/3, Jb 42/11.

(h) <u>Reciprocal</u>

132   The lack of reciprocal pronouns is compensated for by
the use of אָחִיו . . . אִישׁ (Dt 1/16), רֵעֵהוּ . . . אִישׁ (Gn
11/3, 7), or זֶה . . . זֶה (Is 6/3);   cf. § 116. On occasion this may be expressed by the N<u>ip</u>ʿal or H<u>itp</u>ō̄ʿel
themes (cf. §§ 137, 153), or the rare P<u>ō</u>ʿel (cf. § 156).

1. Theme

(a) Qal

133   (i) Stative, expressing a state or condition, e.g. כָּבֵד,
'be heavy,' קָטֹן, 'be small,' מֵת, 'be dead,' בּוֹשׁ,'be
ashamed.'

134   (ii) Fientive, expressing an action, e.g. נָתַן, 'give,'
הָלַךְ, 'go,' שִׂים, 'put.'   *See page 6 for terminology def.*

(b) Niṗ'al

135 ＊(i) Reflexive, e.g. נִשְׁמַר, 'guard oneself,' נִסְתַּר, 'hide
oneself.'

136   (ii) Middle, e.g. נִשְׁאַל, 'ask for oneself,' i.e. 'ask
leave' (I Sm 20/6, 28).   *done for or on behalf of oneself / Not reflected in English*

137 ＊(iii) Reciprocal, e.g. נִשְׁפַּט, 'go to law with one another' (I Sm 12/7), נִלְחַם, 'fight with one another,'
נִצָּה, 'struggle together.'

138   (iv) Tolerative, e.g. נִדְרָשׁ, 'let oneself be consulted'
allowing oneself to be...
(Ezk 14/3).

139 ＊(v) Passive, either of Qal, e.g. נוֹלַד, 'be born,' or of
Pi'el, e.g. נִכְבַּד, 'be honoured.'
Resultative — resulting state. To be "able"   Niph. pct.

(c) Pi'el/Pu'al *passive*

140   As Goetze has demonstrated, the usual description of
these themes as 'intensive' is inaccurate.

To render or Make something ~~~~ to be of the character of the Qal (handwritten)

141　(i) Factitive, with stative verbs, e.g. חִדֵּשׁ, 'restore,'
'renew,' כִּבֵּד, 'honour,' מִלֵּא, 'fill.'

bring about the action denoted by the verb (handwritten)

142　(ii) Causative, with fientive verbs, e.g. יִלֵּד, 'help in
childbirth,' לִמֵּד, 'teach.' This is not a common use.

143　(iii) Plurative or repetitive (perhaps having a separate
origin, with infixed assimilated n?), e.g. שִׁבֵּר, 'smash
to bits,' פִּקֵּשׁ, 'search,' הִלֵּךְ, 'walk about,' 'prowl,'
קִבֵּר, 'bury large numbers,' שָׁאַל, 'beg' (Ps 109/10).

144　(iv) Denominative, i.e. verbs formed from nouns, e.g.

No Qal of these forms (handwritten)

שֵׁרֵשׁ (< שֹׁרֶשׁ), 'root out,' 'uproot,' שָׁלֵשׁ (< שָׁלוֹשׁ), 'do
three times,' 'triple,' כִּהֵן (< כֹּהֵן), 'act as priest.'

depriving: derived from Nouns (handwritten)

145　(v) Privative, i.e. חָטָא, 'sin,' חִטֵּא, 'purify from sin'
(Ps 51/9); סָקַל, 'stone,' סִקֵּל, 'clear of stones" (Is
5/2).

(d) Hip̄ʿîl/Hɔp̄ʿal *- passive* (handwritten)

146　(i) Causative, e.g. הוֹצִיא, 'bring out,' הֶאֱכִיל, 'feed,'
הֶרְאָה, 'show.'

147　(ii) Declarative, e.g. הִצְדִּיק, 'declare righteous,' 'jus-
tify,' הִרְשִׁיעַ, 'declare guilty,' 'condemn.' *Dt. 25:1* (handwritten)

suppose-reported to be (handwritten)

148　(iii) Putative or estimative, e.g. הֵקַל, 'belittle.'

149　(iv) Factitive, although rare, is found with some stative verbs, e.g. הֶלְאָה, 'exhaust,' הֶעֱמִיק, 'deepen,'
הִגְבִּיהַּ, 'make high,' הִקְרִיב, 'bring near,' הֶחֱיָה, 'make
live,' 'revive.'

ingressive (handwritten)

150　(v) Intransitive, a use which indicates the entry into a
state or condition and the remaining in the same, e.g.
הִזְקִין, 'grow old,' הִקְשָׁה, 'become difficult,' הוֹבִישׁ,

30 *ingressive* (handwritten)

'become dry,' הֵמִיק, 'become sweet'; or the exhibiting of a state or quality, e.g. הִשְׂכִּיל, 'act wisely,'
הִרְשִׁיעַ, 'act wickedly,' הֶעֱרִים, 'act craftily.'

151 (vi) Denominative (rarer than Pi'el), e.g. הִשְׁרִישׁ, 'grow
roots' (contrast שֵׁרֵשׁ), הִקְרִין, 'grow horns,' הִלְשִׁין,
'slander' (Pr 30/10), הֵימִין, 'go right,' הִשְׂמְאִיל, 'go
left.'

(e) Hitpō'el

152 (i) Reflexive-iterative, e.g. הִתְהַלֵּךְ, 'walk about' (cf.
French se promener), הִתְחַבֵּא, 'hide oneself,' הִתְפַּלֵּל,
'intercede' (cf. German sich verwenden), הִתְקַדֵּשׁ,
'sanctify oneself.'

153 (ii) Reciprocal-iterative, e.g. הִתְרָאָה, 'look at one
another.'

154 (iii) Reflexive-factitive, e.g. הִתְגַּדֵּל, 'aggrandize
oneself.'

155 (iv) Reflexive-estimative, e.g. הִתְחַלָּה, 'feign illness,'
הִשְׂתָּרֵר, 'regard oneself as a prince,' הִתְנַבֵּא, 'play the
part of a prophet.'

(f) Pō'el

156 Reciprocal, e.g. שׁוֹפֵט, 'be an opponent at law' (Jb
9/15).

2. Voice

(a) Active

157 Expressed by the Qal, Pi'el and Hip̄'īl themes.

31

(b) <u>Middle</u>

158   Expressed by means of the Nip̄‘al theme (cf. § 136).

(c) <u>Passive</u>

159   (i) Passive themes may be employed, viz. <u>Qal</u> passive

ּיֻתַּ֫ן (Nu 32/5; cf. יֻקַּ֫ח, etc.), <u>Nip̄‘al</u>, <u>Pu‘al</u>, <u>Hɔp̄‘al</u>.

160   (ii) Active themes in the impersonal third person sing-

ular or plural may be used, e.g. קָרָא (Gn 11/9), יִתֵּ֫נוּ

(I Kg 18/23).   *obj. of verb become subj. of the passive*

3. Aspect

(a) <u>Perfect</u>

161   (i) Stative, expressing a state or condition. This is

rendered normally by a present tense in English, e.g.

וַאֲנִי זָקַ֫נְתִּי וָשַׂ֫בְתִּי (I Sm 12/2).

162   (ii) Completed action, expressing actions completed

either in reality or in the thought of the speaker.

It may be rendered in English by: (1) a past tense,

e.g. בָּרָא אֱלֹהִים (Gn 1/1); (2) a perfect tense with

'have' denoting action completed in the past but con-

tinuing in its effects into the present, e.g. פֵּרַ֫שְׂתִּי

יָדַי אֵלֶ֫יךָ (Ps 143/6), שָׁבַח אֵל הִסְתִּיר פָּנָיו (Ps 10/11); cf.

Is 1/4; (3) a pluperfect tense to indicate action an-

terior to the accompanying verb, e.g. רָחֵל גְּנָבָתַם,

'Rachel had stolen them' (Gn 31/32); cf. I Sm 9/15,

II Kg 7/17 (note that the subject usually precedes;

cf. § 572, 4); (4) a future perfect tense, e.g. נָתַן

(Dt 8/10), הַדְּחָתִים (Je 8/3).

32

163 (iii) Experience, when a fientive verb expresses a state

of mind, e.g. יָדַעְתִּי, 'I know' (Gn 4/9), זָכַרְנוּ, 'we re-

member' (Nu 11/5), מָאַסְתִּי, 'I despise' (Am 5/21).

164 (iv) Instantaneous action, expressing an act in the pre-

sent which by that very act is completed, e.g. נִשְׁבַּעְתִּי,

'I swear' (Je 22/5), הַעִדֹתִי, 'I testify' (Dt 8/19),

הֲרִימֹתִי, 'I lift up (my hand in an oath)' (Gn 14/22),

אָמַרְתִּי (II Sm 19/30).

165 (v) Certainty (the so-called 'prophetic perfect'), ex-

pressing a vivid future when the action is viewed as

'as good as done,' e.g. הֵן גָּוַעְנוּ אָבַדְנוּ כֻּלָּנוּ אָבָדְנוּ (Nu

17/27; cf. Greek ὅλωλα); cf. Is 5/13.

166 (vi) Conditional. The perfect aspect is employed in un-

real conditions in the past, e.g. לוּ הַחֲיִתֶם אוֹתָם לֹא

הָרַגְתִּי אֶתְכֶם (Ju 8/19); cf. Gn 43/10. It is also used

in expressions of unfulfilled desire, e.g. לוּ־מַתְנוּ

בְּאֶרֶץ מִצְרַיִם, 'If only we had died in the land of Egypt!'

(Nu 14/2), with which contrast לוּ נָמוּת, 'If only we

might die!' (cf. § 174).

(b) Imperfect

167 (i) Incompleted action, either in the present, e.g. מַה־

תְּבַקֵּשׁ (Gn 37/15); cf. I Sm 1/8; or in the past, after

טֶרֶם and בְּטֶרֶם, e.g. טֶרֶם יִשְׁכָּבוּ (Gn 19/4) and עַד, e.g.

וְעַד יִתְקַדְּשׁוּ הַכֹּהֲנִים, 'till the priests had sanctified

themselves' (II Ch 29/34). Thus it may be used for

simple futurity, regularly with statives, but also with

fientives, e.g. וְהֵן לֹא־יַאֲמִינוּ לִי וְלֹא יִשְׁמְעוּ בְּקֹלִי (Ex

33

4/1); cf. Ex 6/1. Sometimes this may involve the future from a past point of view, e.g. שָׁמְע֫וּ כִּי־שָׁם יֹאכְלוּ
לָ֫חֶם, 'They heard that they would have a meal there'
(Gn 43/25); cf. Gn 43/7.

168 (ii) Frequentative or habitual, indicating action repeated either at any time, e.g. כָּ֫כָה יַעֲשֶׂה אִיּוֹב כָּל־הַיָּמִים
(Jb 1/5), כֹּה־יִתֵּן שְׁלֹמֹה לְחִירָם שָׁנָה בְשָׁנָה (I Kg 5/25), or
customarily at a given time, e.g. כַּאֲשֶׁר תַּעֲשֶׂי֫נָה הַדְּבֹרִים
(Dt 1/44), מִכָּל־מַאֲכָל אֲשֶׁר יֵאָכֵל (Gn 6/21), יוֹכְל֫וּן (Gn
43/32). This is specially common in proverbial say-
ings, e.g. בֵּן חָכָם יְשַׂמַּח־אָב (Pr 15/20; the parallel
stich has a participle).

169 (iii) Potential, expressing ability, but less emphatic
than יָכֹל with the infinitive, e.g. אֵיכָה אֶשָּׂא לְבַדִּי (Dt
1/12; cf. לֹא־אוּכַל לְבַדִּי שְׂאֵת אֶתְכֶם in v. 9); cf. II Kg
9/37, Jb 4/17.

170 (iv) Permissive, expressing an idea to be translated by
'may,' e.g. מִכֹּל עֵץ־הַגָּן אָכֹל תֹּאכֵל (Gn 2/16), אֶת־שְׁנֵי בָנַי
תָּמִית אִם־לֹא אֲבִיאֶ֫נּוּ אֵלֶ֫יךָ (Gn 42/37), וְאַחַר דִּבְרִי תַלְעִיג,
'After I have spoken, you may mock' (Jb 21/3).

171 (v) Desiderative, expressing a wish, e.g. הֲתֵלְכִי עִם־הָאִישׁ
הַזֶּה, 'Will you (i.e. do you wish to) go with this
man?' (Gn 24/58), אִם־אֹתָהּ תִּקַּח־לְךָ קָח, 'If you want to
take it, do so' (I Sm 21/10); cf. Ju 4/8.

172 (vi) Obligative, to be rendered by 'ought to,' e.g.
מַעֲשִׂים אֲשֶׁר לֹא־יֵעָשׂוּ עָשִׂיתָ עִמָּדִי, 'You have done things to
me that ought not to be done' (Gn 20/9); cf. Gn 34/7,
Lv 4/13, I Kg 18/27.

173 (vii) Injunctive, expressing a strong command, to be
rendered by 'must,' 'shall,' 'are to,' etc., e.g. עַל־
גְּחֹנְךָ תֵלֵךְ וְעָפָר תֹּאכַל (Gn 3/14); cf. Ex 21/12. With
the negative particle לֹא it expresses prohibition
(which is stronger than the vetitive, cf. § 186), e.g.
Ex 20/13-17.

174 (viii) Conditional. The imperfect aspect is used in
real conditions in the future, e.g. אִם־אֶצְדַּק פִּי
יַרְשִׁיעֵנִי (Jb 9/20), כִּי־אֵלֵךְ בְּגֵיא צַלְמָוֶת (Ps 23/4), or
desire with לוּ, e.g. לוּ שָׁקוֹל יִשָּׁקֵל כַּעְשִׂי (Jb 6/2; contrast § 166).

175 (ix) The imperfect aspect is employed after telic particles, viz. לְמַעַן (אֲשֶׁר) (cf. § 367), e.g. Gn 12/13,
Je 42/6; פֶּן (cf. § 461), e.g. Gn 3/3; לְבִלְתִּי (cf.
§ 424), e.g. Ex 20/20; בַּעֲבוּר (cf. § 521), e.g. Gn
27/4; אֲשֶׁר (cf. § 466), e.g. Dt 4/40.

(c) <u>Preterite</u>

176 This was originally a true past tense, as in Ugaritic
whln.ʻnt.lbth.tmġyn / tštql.ỉlt.lhklh / wl.šbʻt.tmtḫsh.
bʻmq, 'See! Anat proceeded to her house, the goddess
started for her palace; but she was not sated with her
fighting in the valley' (<u>UTB</u>, ʻnt II.iii.17-19) and in
Moabite עמרי מלך ישראל ויעגו את מאב ימן רבן כי יאנף כמש
בארצה, 'Omri, king of Israel, oppressed Moab for a long
time, because Chemosh was angry with his land' (<u>KAI</u>,
181/4-6); cf. also Akkadian <u>iprus</u>.

177 In classical Hebrew this form is preserved in archaic

(poetic) language, e.g. נָטִיתָ || תִּבְלָעֵמוֹ (Ex 15/12; cf. 14 f.), אִוָּלֶד (Jb 3/3; cf. 11); cf. Dt 32/10, Is 5/12, 9/17. It occurs in prose after אָז, e.g. אָז יַקְהֵל שְׁלֹמֹה (I Kg 8/1), אָז יָשִׁיר־מֹשֶׁה (Ex 15/1); cf. Dt 4/41, Nu 21/17, Jo 8/30, 10/12 (note that the perfect aspect is found in Gn 4/26, Jo 10/33, II Kg 14/8). This is the form which occurs with the waw-'consecutive,' from which use, by analogy, came the construction waw-'consecutive' plus perfect.

(d) Consecution

    (i) 'Consecutive' waw expressing temporal sequence (cf. § 495) or result (cf. § 524).

178   (1) 'Consecutive' waw and the 'imperfect,' originally the preterite with the early pronunciation of the conjunction retained as wa-, now equivalent to the perfect aspect, e.g. וְהַמַּיִם גָּבְרוּ מְאֹד מְאֹד עַל־הָאָרֶץ וַיְכֻסּוּ כָּל־הֶהָרִים (Gn 7/19); cf. Gn 18/7, I Sm 15/20.

179   (2) By analogy, waw occurs with the perfect. Since it is a later development, the conjunction has the normal later vowel reduction, becoming wᵉ-. This is an equivalent of the imperfect aspect, e.g. פֶּן־יֶחְדַּל אָבִי מִן־הָאֲתֹנוֹת וְדָאַג לָנוּ (I Sm 9/5); cf. Gn 18/18, 24/4.

    (ii) 'Simple' waw.

180   (1) Sometimes this occurs with the imperfect aspect as a simple imperfect, e.g. וַאֲפִיצֵם (Gn 49/7); cf. Is 5/29. This seems to be confined to poetry (an ex-

ception is I Kg 18/27).

181   (2) 'Simple' waw with the precative expresses purpose
       (cf. §§ 187,517), e.g. וָאֶעֱשֶׂה עִמּוֹ חֶסֶד (II Sm 9/1),
       or occasionally a command (cf. § 185), e.g. וִיהִי־נָא
       פִּי־שְׁנַיִם בְּרוּחֲךָ אֵלָי (II Kg 2/9).

182   (3) 'Simple' waw with the perfect occurs in classical
       Hebrew when two or more verbs follow in a closely
       related series, e.g. הוּא הֵסִיר אֶת־הַבָּמוֹת וְשִׁבַּר אֶת־
       הַמַּצֵּבֹת וְכָרַת אֶת־הָאֲשֵׁרָה וְכִתַּת נְחַשׁ הַנְּחֹשֶׁת (II Kg 18/4);
       cf. II Kg 21/6, 23/4 f., II Sm 7/9-13. A clear ex-
       ception is וְהִרְאַנִי (II Kg 8/10);   examples such as
       וְנָעַל (II Sm 13/18), וְהִכָּה (I Kg 20/21), should per-
       haps be vocalized as absolute infinitives (cf.
       § 210).   In late usage the waw-'consecutive' con-
       struction breaks down, e.g. וְנָתַתִּי אֶת־לִבִּי לִדְרוֹשׁ
       וְלָתוּר בַּחָכְמָה (Ec 1/13);   cf. Ec 2/12 f.

                          4. Mood

   (a) Precative

183   This is identical in form, though not in origin, with
   the preterite.

184   (i) Optative, expressing a strong desire or wish (cf.
       § 545), e.g. יְחִי הַמֶּלֶךְ (I Sm 10/24), יָקָם /י אֶת־הַבְרוֹ
       (I Sm 1/23), אֹכְלָה בָשָׂר (Dt 12/20);   cf. Dt 17/14. For
       negation אַל is used, e.g. אַל־אֶרְאֶה בְּמוֹת הַיֶּלֶד (Gn 21/16);
       cf. Je 17/18.

185   (ii) Jussive and cohortative, expressing a command in

                              37

the third and first persons respectively, e.g. נֵלְכָ֫ה

וְנַֽעַבְדָה אֱלֹהִים אֲחֵרִים (Dt 13/7); cf. Ju 15/2. Sometimes

this occurs after 'simple' waw when purpose is not in-

tended (cf. § 181), e.g. וְיִתְּנוּ־לָ֫נוּ שְׁנַ֫יִם פָּרִים וְיִבְחֲרוּ

וְיִֽנַתְּחֻ֫הוּ וְיָשִׂ֫ימוּ עַל־הָעֵצִים . . . (I Kg 18/23); cf. II Kg

2/9.

186 (iii) Vetitive, the negative of the imperative (cf.

§ 188), is expressed by אַל with the second person of

the precative, e.g. זְכֹר אַל־תִּשְׁכַּח (Dt 9/7); cf. I Kg

13/22.

187 (iv) Purpose, employed after 'simple' waw in telic

clauses (cf. §§ 517, 181), e.g. וְהָבִ֫יאָה לִּי וְאֹכֵ֫לָה (Gn

27/4); cf. I Kg 21/2.

(b) Imperative

188 (i) Command, in the second person only; otherwise the

precative must be used (cf. § 185), as also for the

vetitive (cf. § 186).

189 (ii) Purpose may occasionally be intended when two im-

peratives are joined by waw (cf. § 518), e.g. לְכִי

אִיעָצֵךְ נָא עֵצָה וּמַלְּטִי אֶת־נַפְשֵׁךְ (I Kg 1/12); cf. II Kg

5/10, II Sm 21/3.

190 (iii) A conditional meaning can also be expressed by

two imperatives joined by waw, e.g. זֹאת עֲשׂוּ וִֽחְיוּ (Gn

42/18); cf. Is 36/16.

191 (iv) Interjectional, when employed in the singular as a

particle, e.g. קוּם (Ex 32/1), הָ֫בָה (Gn 11/3, 7), לְכָה

(Gn 19/32).

5. Verbal Nouns

(a) Construct Infinitive

192 (i) As subject of a sentence, e.g. לֹא־טֹוב הֱיֹות הָאָדָם
לְבַדֹּו (Gn 2/18); cf. I Sm 18/23. It may be accompanied by the introducing לְ (cf. § 276), e.g. וְאִם רַע
בְּעֵינֵיכֶם לַעֲבֹד אֶת־י׳ (Jo 24/15).

193 (ii) As object of a verb, e.g. לֹא אֵדַע צֵאת וָבֹא (I Kg
3/7); cf. Dt 10/10; also with the introducing לְ (cf.
§ 276), e.g. לֹא־נְתַתִּיךָ לִנְגֹּעַ אֵלֶיהָ (Gn 20/6). This may
even occur with the accusative particle: וְאֵת הִתְרַגֶּזְךָ
אֵלָי (II Kg 19/27 = Is 37/28).

194 (iii) As a genitive, e.g. בְּיֹום אֲכָלְךָ מִמֶּנּוּ (Gn 2/17); cf.
Gn 29/7. So always after prepositions (cf. § 36).

195 (iv) As a gerund, with לְ of norm (cf. § 274), to be rendered 'by . . .-ing,' e.g. וְשָׁמְרוּ בְנֵי־יִשְׂרָאֵל אֶת־הַשַּׁבָּת
לַעֲשֹׂות אֶת־הַשַּׁבָּת לְדֹרֹתָם בְּרִית עֹולָם (Ex 31/16); cf. I Sm
14/33, 12/17; so לֵאמֹר (Ex 5/19). The negative em-
ploys לְבִלְתִּי (cf. § 423), e.g. הִשָּׁמֶר לְךָ פֶּן־תִּשְׁכַּח אֶת־י׳
אֱלֹהֶיךָ לְבִלְתִּי שְׁמֹר מִצְוֹתָיו (Dt 8/11). The meaning is similar to Latin (ad) portandi/um/ō (especially in the
ablative).

196 (v) As a gerundive, with לְ of product (cf. § 278), to be
rendered 'is to be . . .-ed,' e.g. מֶה לַעֲשֹׂות לָךְ הֲיֵשׁ
לְדַבֶּר־לָךְ אֶל־הַמֶּלֶךְ (II Kg 4/13); cf. Gn 15/12, Jo 2/5,
Es 3/14. The negative is expressed by לֹא (cf. § 397),
e.g. לֹא לְהַזְכִּיר בְּשֵׁם י׳ (Am 6/10), or, in late usage, by
אֵין (cf. § 410), e.g. וַיָּבֹוא עַד לִפְנֵי שַׁעַר־הַמֶּלֶךְ כִּי אֵין

לָבוֹא אֶל־שַׁעַר הַמֶּלֶךְ בִּלְבוּשׁ שָׂק (Es 4/2). This is similar in meaning to Latin _portandus est_.

197   (vi) Purpose, with לְ (cf. § 277), לְמַעַן (cf. § 367), or בַּעֲבוּר (cf. § 521), and in the negative with לְבִלְתִּי (cf. § 424).

198   (vii) Consequence or result, with לְ (cf. § 279), to be rendered 'thus . . .-ing,' e.g. לְהַכְעִיסוֹ (Dt 4/25); cf. Nu 11/11, Lv 20/3, I Kg 2/27; or else 'so . . . that . . .,' e.g. מַדּוּעַ מָצָאתִי חֵן בְּעֵינֶיךָ לְהַכִּירֵנִי (Ru 2/10). Rarely לְמַעַן is used (cf. § 368), e.g. לְמַעַן חַלֵּל אֶת־שֵׁם קָדְשִׁי (Am 2/7); cf. II Kg 22/17.

199   (viii) Degree, with לְ (cf. § 275), to be rendered 'enough to . . .,' e.g. וַיֵּצֶר לְאַמְנוֹן לְהִתְחַלּוֹת בַּעֲבוּר תָּמָר אֲחֹתוֹ (II Sm 13/2); cf. Dt 9/20, II Kg 20/1.

200   (ix) Frequently after prepositions, especially with temporal (cf. §§ 502-507), causal (cf. § 534), or concessive (cf. § 530 f.) meaning.

(b) Absolute Infinitive

201   Of different origin to the construct infinitive, it normally takes neither prefixes nor suffixes (note, however, § 207).

202   (i) As subject of a sentence (confined to poetry), e.g. הַכֵּר־פָּנִים בְּמִשְׁפָּט בַּל־טוֹב (Pr 24/23); cf. Jb 6/25.

203   (ii) As object of a verb, e.g. לֹא־יִתְּנֵנִי הָשֵׁב רוּחִי (Jb 9/18); cf. Dt 28/56, Is 1/17.

204   (iii) In the adverbial accusative of manner (cf. § 60), e.g. וַיִּגַּשׁ (Dt 13/15), וְשָׁאַלְתָּ הֵיטֵב (Jo 2/5), רָדְפוּ מַהֵר

וַתֵּשֶׁב לָהּ מִנֶּגֶד הַרְחֵק (Gn 21/16), הַפְּלִשְׁתִּי הַשְׁכֵּם וְהַעֲרֵב (I Sm 17/16), הָחֵל וְכַלֵּה (I Sm 3/12).

205 (iv) To indicate emphasis, the absolute infinitive precedes the finite form of the same root (but not neces-
sarily the same theme), e.g. מוֹת תָּמוּת (Gn 2/17), טָרֹף
טֹרַף (Gn 44/28); cf. Am 9/8, Jb 6/2, Ex 21/12. Instances of this construction in Ugaritic reveal that
the infinitive was in the nominative case, e.g. hm ǵmu
ǵmit (UTB, 51.iv.34); so with following infinitive:
yspi spu (UTB, 121.ii.10). In Hebrew the infinitive
may occasionally follow, e.g. יָצֹא יָצוֹא (II Kg 5/11);
so always with an imperative, e.g. הָרְגֵנִי נָא הָרֹג (Nu
11/15). This infinitive normally precedes a negative,
e.g. וְהָמֵת אַל־תְּמִיתֵהוּ (Ju 1/28), וְהוֹרֵשׁ לֹא הוֹרִישׁוֹ (I Kg
3/26); cf. Ju 15/13, Is 30/19. It may, however, fol-
low, e.g. לֹא הַשְׁמֵיד אַשְׁמִיד (Am 9/8); cf. Ps 49/8, Gn 3/4.

206 (v) To express continuous action or repetition it follows the finite verb, and is often of the same root,
e.g. וַיֹּאכַל גַּם־אָכוֹל (Gn 31/15); cf. Nu 11/32. This is
especially common with a second infinitive, e.g. הָלְכוּ
הָלֹךְ וְגָעוֹ (I Sm 6/12); cf. Ju 14/9, Gn 8/3, 5; or
with an adjective, e.g. וַיֵּלֶךְ הָלוֹךְ וְרָב (I Sm 14/19), or
participle, e.g. וַיֵּלֶךְ הָלוֹךְ וְקָרֵב (II Sm 18/25).

207 (vi) As a genitive (rare), e.g. מִדֶּרֶךְ הַשְׂכֵּל (Pr 21/16);
cf. Is 14/23. So also exceptionally after prepositions: לְהֵרָאֹה (Ju 13/21, I Sm 3/21), עַד־כַּלֵּה (II Kg
13/17, 19), וְאַחֲרֵי שָׁתֹה (I Sm 1/9).

208 (vii) As a substitute for a finite verb (cf. French voir,

and the Greek infinitive of command):

209   (1) For the imperfect, e.g. רָגוֹם אֹתוֹ בָאֲבָנִים כָּל־הָעֵדָה
        (Nu 15/35); cf. Nu 30/3, Dt 15/2, II Kg 4/43, Gn
        17/10, Ex 12/48.

210   (2) For the perfect, e.g. וְנָפוֹץ הַכַּדִּים אֲשֶׁר בְּיָדָם (Ju
        7/19); cf. I Sm 2/28, Gn 41/43, Es 3/13, Ps 17/5.
        Thus the absolute infinitive sometimes precedes an
        independent personal pronoun, as frequently in Phoen-
        ician, e.g. קרא אנך (KAI, 10/2); cf. KAI, 26A 1/6,
        11; so in Hebrew וְשַׁבֵּחַ אֲנִי (Ec 4/2); cf. Es 9/1.

211   (3) For the imperative, e.g. הָלוֹךְ וְרָחַצְתָּ (II Kg 5/10);
        cf. Is 14/31 (parallel to an imperative).

212   (4) For the precative, e.g. פָּגוֹשׁ דֹּב שַׁכּוּל בְּאִישׁ וְאַל־
        כְּסִיל בְּאִוַּלְתּוֹ (Pr 17/12); cf. Lv 6/7.

   (c) Participle

213 (i) To express continuous action, either in the present,
     e.g. אֶת־אַחַי אָנֹכִי מְבַקֵּשׁ (Gn 37/16); cf. Gn 3/5, I Sm
     23/1, II Kg 7/9; or in the past, e.g. רַק בַּבָּמוֹת הוּא
     מְזַבֵּחַ וּמַקְטִיר (I Kg 3/3); cf. Jb 1/14. The verb הָיָה
     sometimes accompanies the participle in such expres-
     sions of duration, e.g. וְהַנַּעַר הָיָה מְשָׁרֵת אֶת־י' (I Sm
     2/11); cf. Ju 16/21, II Kg 17/25.

214 (ii) To indicate imminent action, e.g. וַאֲנִי הִנְנִי מֵבִיא
     אֶת־הַמַּבּוּל (Gn 6/17); cf. Gn 20/3, I Kg 20/13.

215 (iii) Adjectival, either attributive, e.g. אֵשׁ אֹכְלָה (Dt
     4/24), or predicative, e.g. אִישׁ יֹצֵא (Ju 1/24).

216 (iv) In a gerundive or admissive sense, meaning 'may be

. . .,' 'is to be . . .' This is usually the Niph'al

theme, e.g. נִכְבָּד, 'honourable,' נוֹרָא, 'terrible,' נֶחְמָד,

'desirable,' נֶאֱמָן, 'dependable,' נִתְעָב, 'detestable,'

but the Pu'al may also be used, e.g. מְהֻלָּל, 'laudable,'

'praiseworthy.'

217 (v) Substantival, e.g. אוֹיֵב, 'enemy,' חֹזֶה, 'seer,' רֹעֶה,

'shepherd,' שֹׁמֵר, 'watchman, spy.'

218 (vi) As equivalent to a relative clause, with the ar-

ticle (cf. § 90), e.g. הַנֹּגֵעַ בָּאִישׁ הַזֶּה (Gn 26/11); cf.

Gn 12/7, Ju 6/28.

219 (vii) In circumstantial clauses (cf. § 494), e.g. וְלוֹט

יֹשֵׁב בְּשַׁעַר־סְדֹם (Gn 19/1), וְאֵינֶנּוּ אֹכֵל לָחֶם (I Kg 21/5).

220 (viii) To express simultaneous action (synchronism; cf.

§§ 236 f.), e.g. וֶאֱלִישָׁע רֹאֶה וְהוּא מְצַעֵק (II Kg 2/12);

cf. II Kg 4/5, I Sm 25/20.

221 (ix) To indicate repetition or continuous action (like

the absolute infinitive; cf. § 206), e.g. וְדָוִד עֹלֶה

בְמַעֲלֵה הַזֵּיתִים עֹלֶה וּבוֹכֶה (II Sm 15/30); cf. I Sm 17/41,

Ex 19/19.

222 (x) To express an indefinite subject, e.g. כִּי־יִפֹּל הַנֹּפֵל

מִמֶּנּוּ (Dt 22/8); cf. II Sm 17/9, Am 9/1, Je 9/23.

6. Verbal Co-ordination

223 In this construction, the second verb usually expresses

the principal idea, while the first indicates the manner,

and may conveniently be rendered in translation by the use

of an adverb.

43

(a) Two Finite Verbs

224   (i) With the conjunction, e.g. וַיָּ֫שָׁב וַיִּשְׁכַּב, 'he lay down again' (I Kg 19/6), וַיַּשְׁכֵּם יְהוֹשֻׁעַ בַּבֹּ֫קֶר וַיִּפְקֹד אֶת־הָעָם, 'Joshua mustered the people first thing in the morning' (Jo 8/10); cf. Gn 25/1, 24/18, Jo 8/14.

225   (ii) Asyndetic (usually confined to poetry), e.g. לֹא אוֹסִיף עוֹד אֲרַחֵם (Ho 1/6); cf. I Sm 2/3, Ps 106/13, Zp 3/7; for a prose example cf. Gn 30/31. But imperatives may be asyndetic even in prose, e.g. שׁוּב שְׁכָב (I Sm 3/5 f.).

(b) Finite Verb with Infinitive

226   The infinitive usually has the introducing לְ (cf. § 276), e.g. לָ֫מָּה נַחְבֵּ֫אתָ לִבְרֹחַ, 'Why did you run away furtively?' (Gn 31/27), הִקְשִׁ֫יתָ לִשְׁאוֹל, 'You have made a difficult request' (II Kg 2/10); cf. I Sm 15/12, Ps 126/2 f.; however, the preposition may be omitted, e.g. מַדּ֫וּעַ מִהַרְתֶּן בֹּא הַיּוֹם, 'Why have you come so quickly today?' (Ex 2/18); cf. Nu 22/15, I Sm 3/6, 8.

7.   Concord of Subject and Verb

227   (a) When the subject precedes, the verb normally exhibits concord of gender and number, e.g. וְתַרְדֵּמָה נָפְלָה עַל־אַבְרָם (Gn 15/12).

228   (b) When the verb precedes, the third masculine singular of the verb is often used regardless of the gender or number of the subject, especially when the latter is inanimate or animal, e.g. . . . יְהִי מְאֹרֹת בִּרְקִ֫יעַ הַשָּׁמַ֫יִם.

44

וְהָיוּ לְאֹתֹת (Gn 1/14); cf. Gn 39/5, II Kg 3/18, 26;
note that the following verbs exhibit concord. An example with a human subject is וַיֹּאמֶר שָׂרֵי סֻכּוֹת (Ju 8/6).

229 (c) Collectives often take the plural of the verb _ad
sensum, e.g. וַיָּנֻסוּ אֲרָם (I Kg 20/20); cf. I Kg 18/24,
Jb 1/14, I Sm 17/46.

230 (d) Compound subjects usually take the verb in the singular when the latter precedes, and in the plural when
it follows, e.g. וַתַּעַן רָחֵל וְלֵאָה וַתֹּאמַרְנָה לוֹ (Gn 31/14);
cf. Nu 12/1 f., I Sm 19/18, II Kg 3/9.

231 (e) Dual subjects normally have the verb in the plural,
e.g. תֶּחֱזַקְנָה יָדֶיךָ (Ju 7/11).

232 (f) Subjects in the plural of respect (cf. § 8) take the
verb normally in the singular, e.g. אִם־אֲדֹנָיו יִתֶּן־לוֹ
אִשָּׁה (Ex 21/4); cf. Ex 21/29.

233 (g) Abstract plural subjects (cf. § 7) may have the verb
in the singular, e.g. תִּתְחַדֵּשׁ כַּנֶּשֶׁר נְעוּרָיְכִי (Ps 103/5).

234 (h) Second feminine plural forms of verbs are rare, and
are usually replaced by the masculine, e.g. כַּאֲשֶׁר עֲשִׂיתֶם
(Ru 1/8); cf. Am 4/1, Jl 2/22. Similarly the masculine is used for the third feminine plural imperfect,
e.g. וְשֶׁבַע הַפָּרוֹת . . . יִהְיוּ שֶׁבַע שְׁנֵי רָעָב (Gn 41/27),
especially when the verb precedes, e.g. אִם־יֵצְאוּ בְנוֹת־
שִׁילוֹ (Ju 21/21); cf. I Kg 11/3, II Sm 4/1.

8. Synchronism (Simultaneous Action)

235 (a) Indicated by two perfects with the subjects preced-

ing, the first subject being asyndetic, e.g. הֵמָּה בָאוּ

בְאֶרֶץ צוּף וְשָׁאוּל אָמַר לְנַעֲרוֹ (I Sm 9/5); cf. Gn 44/3 f.,

Ju 15/14. This may even be accompanied by a negative,

e.g. יְשַׁעְיָהוּ לֹא יָצָא הָעִיר הַתִּיכֹנָה וּדְבַר־י' הָיָה אֵלָיו (II Kg

20/4).

236 (b) Indicated by two participles, with subjects preced-

ing, the first asyndetic (cf. § 220; but note II Kg

2/12 with introductory <u>waw</u>!), e.g. הֵמָּה בָּאִים בְּתוֹךְ הָעִיר

וְהִנֵּה שְׁמוּאֵל יֹצֵא לִקְרָאתָם (I Sm 9/14); cf. II Kg 8/5,

I Sm 25/20.

237 (c) Indicated by a participle and a perfect, with sub-

jects preceding, the first asyndetic, e.g. הֵמָּה עֹלִים

בְּמַעֲלֵה הָעִיר וְהֵמָּה מָצְאוּ נְעָרוֹת (I Sm 9/11); cf. I Sm

9/27.

46

1. Prepositions

238   When a preposition governs more than one object, it is normal to repeat it before each one, e.g. לֶךְ־לְךָ מֵאַרְצְךָ וּמִמּוֹלַדְתְּךָ וּמִבֵּית אָבִיךָ (Gn 12/1); cf. Ho 2/21. However, this is not always the case, e.g. הַחֵפֶץ לַי׳ בְּעֹלוֹת וּזְבָחִים (I Sm 15/22).

239   (a) בְּ, expressing rest or movement in place or time.

240   (i) Locative, e.g. בַּבַּיִת, 'in the house,' בָּאָרֶץ, 'in/ through the land,' בָּהָר, 'on the mountain.'

241   (ii) Temporal, expressing point of time, e.g. בַּבֹּקֶר (with which contrast the temporal accusative, § 56). It may be used also with an infinitive (cf. § 503), e.g. בְּהִבָּרְאָם (Gn 2/4), or with a noun clause (cf. § 498), e.g. בְּעוֹד שְׁלֹשָׁה חֳדָשִׁים לַקָּצִיר (Am 4/7).

242   (iii) Adversative, expressing disadvantage, e.g. יָדוֹ בַכֹּל וְיַד כֹּל בּוֹ (Gn 16/12); cf. I Sm 18/17. Sometimes this is to be rendered 'in spite of,' e.g. לֹא־יַאֲמִינוּ בִי בְּכֹל הָאֹתוֹת אֲשֶׁר עָשִׂיתִי בְּקִרְבּוֹ (Nu 14/11); cf. Is 9/11.

243   (iv) Means or instrument, e.g. פֶּן־יִפְגָּעֵנוּ בַּדֶּבֶר אוֹ בֶחָרֶב (Ex 5/3); cf. Ex 16/3, Mi 4/14.

244   (v) Transitivity, in the completion of some verbs where the preposition really expresses means, but

an accusative is normal, e.g. וְאָנִיעָה עֲלֵיכֶם בְּמוֹ רֹאשִׁי
(Jb 16/4; contrast Ps 22/8), פָּעֲרוּ עָלַי בְּפִיהֶם (Jb 16/10;
contrast Jb 29/23); cf. Pr 6/13 (contrast Pr 10/10),
Ps 46/7, Ex 7/20.

245 (vi) Agent (rare, usually expressed by לְ, cf. § 280),
     e.g. שֹׁפֵךְ דַּם הָאָדָם בָּאָדָם דָּמוֹ יִשָּׁפֵךְ (Gn 9/6); cf. Nu 36/2.

246 (vii) Price or exchange, e.g. תְּנָה־לִּי אֶת־כַּרְמְךָ בְּכֶסֶף (I Kg
     21/6); cf. I Kg 10/29. Sometimes this is to be ren-
     dered 'at the risk/peril of,' e.g. הֲדַם הָאֲנָשִׁים הַהֹלְכִים
     בְּנַפְשׁוֹתָם (II Sm 23/17); cf. I Kg 2/23.

247 (viii) Causal, e.g. הֲתַשְׁחִית בַּחֲמִשָּׁה אֶת־כָּל־הָעִיר (Gn 18/28);
     so with an infinitive (cf. § 534), e.g. בַּעֲזָבְכֶם אֶת־מִצְוֺת
     /י (I Kg 18/18) or a noun clause (cf. § 533), e.g.
     בַּאֲשֶׁר אַתְּ־אִשְׁתּוֹ (Gn 39/9); cf. Gn 39/23.

248 (ix) Accompaniment, e.g. וַתָּבֹא יְרוּשָׁלְַמָה בְּחַיִל כָּבֵד (I Kg
     10/2); cf. Gn 9/4, I Kg 19/19, Ex 10/9.

249 (x) Identity (essentiae), with a predicate, explicative
     of some noun in the clause (cf. French agir en témoin,
     déguisé en pélerin), e.g. כִּי־אֱלֹהֵי אָבִי בְּעֶזְרִי (Ex 18/4),
     בִּמְתֵי מְעָט (Dt 26/5, 28/62); cf. Ex 6/3.

250 (xi) Specification, indicating the parts of which the
     whole consists, e.g. וַיִּגְוַע כָּל־בָּשָׂר הָרֹמֵשׂ עַל־הָאָרֶץ בָּעוֹף
     וּבַבְּהֵמָה וּבַחַיָּה וּבְכָל־הַשֶּׁרֶץ (Gn 7/21); cf. Ex 12/19, 13/2.

251 (xii) Partitive, e.g. וְנָשְׂאוּ אִתְּךָ בְּמַשָּׂא הָעָם (Nu 11/17);
     cf. II Kg 17/25.

252 (xiii) Norm, expressing a state or condition, e.g.
     בְּשָׁלוֹם (Gn 15/15), בְּתֻמּוֹ (Pr 19/1), בְּצֶדֶק (Lv 19/15),
     בְּרָעָה (Ex 32/12).

253   (xiv) Pregnant, with verbs of motion, expressing move-
        ment <u>to</u> resulting in rest <u>in</u> a place, e.g. אֶת־ וְשִׁלַּח
        הַשָּׂעִיר בַּמִּדְבָּר (Lv 16/22);   cf. I Kg 11/2, Gn 19/8.

254   (xv) Distributive (cf. § 102), e.g. יוֹם בְּיוֹם (II Ch
        30/21), שָׁנָה בְשָׁנָה (I Sm 1/7);   cf. Ne 8/18, I Sm
        18/10, Ez 3/4, I Ch 27/1.

255   (b) כְּ, expressing likeness, which may be either simil-
      arity or identity.

256   (i) Comparative, e.g. הֲנִהְיָה כַּדָּבָר הַגָּדוֹל הַזֶּה (Dt 4/32);
        with an infinitive, וַיְשַׁסְּעֵהוּ כְּשַׁסַּע הַגְּדִי (Ju 14/6);
        cf. II Sm 3/34. When used in a hypothetical sense
        this must be rendered 'as if,' 'as it were,' e.g.
        כְּהָנִיף שֵׁבֶט אֶת־מְרִימָיו כְּהָרִים מַטֶּה לֹא־עֵץ (Is 10/15).   It
        may also be used with a clause introduced by אֲשֶׁר,
        e.g. וְאֶתְּנָה כַּאֲשֶׁר תֹּאמְרוּ אֵלָי (Gn 34/12).   The meaning
        'such . . . as' may be expressed in several ways,
        e.g. כַּדָּבָר הַזֶּה (Gn 44/7), גּוֹי אֲשֶׁר־כָּזֶה (Je 5/9), הֲנִמְצָא
        כָזֶה אִישׁ (Gn 41/38).   The preposition may be repeated
        to express the meaning 'the same as,' e.g. כְּכֹחִי אָז
        וּכְכֹחִי עָתָּה (Jo 14/11);   cf. Gn 18/25, I Kg 22/4,
        II Sm 11/25.

257   (ii) Approximation, with numerals, e.g. וַיֵּשְׁבוּ שָׁם כְּעֶשֶׂר
        שָׁנִים (Ru 1/4);   cf. Ex 12/37, I Sm 9/22.

258   (iii) Concessive, with an infinitive (cf. § 531), e.g.
        וַיְהִי כְּדַבְּרָהּ אֶל־יוֹסֵף יוֹם יוֹם (Gn 39/10).

259   (iv) Norm, meaning 'in accordance with,' e.g. אִישׁ
        כִּלְבָבוֹ (I Sm 13/14), כַּמִּשְׁפָּט (II Kg 11/14), כְּחַסְדְּךָ (Ps

51/3).

260 (v) Causal, before clauses introduced by כַּאֲשֶׁר, meaning
properly 'in accordance with the fact that . . .'
(cf. § 533), e.g. כַּאֲשֶׁר לֹא־שָׁמַעְתָּ בְּקוֹל יְ (I Sm 28/18);
cf. II Kg 17/26, Nu 27/14, Ju 6/27.

261 (vi) Asseverative, expressing identity, e.g. כִּי־הוּא
כְאִישׁ אֱמֶת, 'for he is a truly honest man' (Ne 7/2),
וְשַׂמְתִּיךְ כְּרֹאִי, 'I will make you a veritable gazing-
stock' (Na 3/6); cf. II Sm 9/8, I Sm 20/3, Jb 10/9,
Nu 11/1.

262 (vii) Temporal, expressing exact point of time, to be
rendered 'as soon as,' 'at the very time,' e.g. כָּעֵת
מָחָר (I Sm 9/16); cf. Gn 18/10, 14; with an infinitive (cf. § 504), e.g. וַיְהִי כְּבוֹא אַבְרָם מִצְרַיְמָה (Gn
12/14). With a clause introduced by כַּאֲשֶׁר or שֶׁ the
meaning has weakened to a mere 'when' (cf. § 499),
e.g. כַּאֲשֶׁר אָמְרוּ (I Sm 8/6), כְּשֶׁתִּפּוֹל עֲלֵיהֶם פִּתְאֹם (Ec
9/12). The form כְּמוֹ may be followed by a clause
without an introductory particle, e.g. וּכְמוֹ הַשַּׁחַר עָלָה
(Gn 19/15).

263 (viii) Pregnant, resulting from an ellipsis of another
preposition, e.g. of בְּ in כִּי כְהַר־פְּרָצִים יָקוּם יְ כְּעֵמֶק
עַד אֲשֶׁר־גְּנִיחַ יְ בְּגִבְעוֹן יִרְגָּז (Is 28/21), and of לְ in
לַאֲחִיכֶם כָּכֶם (Jo 1/15). But contrast כַּבָּרִאשֹׁנָה (Ju
20/32).

264 (ix) Degree, with a noun clause introduced by כַּאֲשֶׁר and
followed by כֵּן, with the meaning 'the more . . . the
more,' e.g. וְכַאֲשֶׁר יְעַנּוּ אֹתוֹ כֵּן יִרְבֶּה (Ex 1/12).

50

265   (c) לְ, expressing motion towards a thing or person, or
      relation to something.

266   (i) Terminative in space or time, to be rendered 'to,'
         'up to,' e.g. לָעִיר (I Sm 9/12), לְאֶלֶף דּוֹר (Dt 7/9),
         לְעוֹלָם (II Kg 5/27).

267   (ii) Directive, meaning 'towards,' e.g. לְאָחוֹר, 'back-
         wards' (Je 7/24), לְמַעְלָה, 'upwards' (Ezk 8/2), לְעֵבֶר
         אֶחָד (I Sm 14/40).

268   (iii) Temporal, meaning 'towards,' 'by,' e.g. וְהָיֵה
         נָכוֹן לַבֹּקֶר וְעָלִיתָ בַבֹּקֶר אֶל־הַר סִינַי, 'Be ready by the
         morning, and come up in the morning to Mount Sinai'
         (Ex 34/2); cf. Ps 90/6, Ex 19/11, II Kg 4/16, Gn
         17/21. In late texts לְ may take the place of a tem-
         poral accusative (cf. § 56), expressing duration of
         time, e.g. לְשָׁנִים שָׁלוֹשׁ (II Ch 11/17); cf. II Ch
         29/17.

269   (iv) Indirect object, e.g. וַיִּתֶּן־לוֹ צֹאן וּבָקָר (Gn 24/35).

270   (v) Possessive, e.g. וַיִּרְאוּ הַצֹּפִים לְשָׁאוּל (I Sm 14/16);
         cf. II Kg 5/9. This is required when the possessor
         is definite but the object possessed indefinite,
         e.g. הִנֵּה רָאִיתִי בֵּן לְיִשַׁי (I Sm 16/18); cf. I Kg 18/22,
         Dt 5/9.

271   (vi) Interest, expressing either advantage, e.g. אָרָה־
         לִּי אֶת־הָעָם הַזֶּה (Nu 22/6); cf. Nu 23/1; or disadvan-
         tage, e.g. מִתְאַנֶּה הוּא לִי (II Kg 5/7); cf. I Sm 9/20
         (לְךָ), Ju 12/5.

272   (vii) Reflexive, restricted to the same person as the
         subject of the verb (unlike the לְ of interest), and

51

especially common with verbs of motion, e.g. לֶךְ־לְךָ (Gn
12/1), שׁוּבוּ לָכֶם (Dt 5/30);   cf. Nu 22/34, Gn 21/16.

273   (viii) Specification, meaning 'with respect to,' e.g.
לֹא־רָאִיתִי כָהֵנָּה . . . לָרֹעַ and לָכֵן (Gn 41/19);   cf. Dt
5/8, I Sm 9/20. Sometimes this takes the place of the
accusative of specification (cf. § 57), e.g. וְנִסְלַח לוֹ
(Lv 4/26), leading to the use of לְ with a substantive
as a variant of the accusative of the direct object of
a verb, e.g. לְשַׁחֵת לָעִיר בַּעֲבוּרִי (I Sm 23/10);   cf. Dt
9/27, Am 8/9, Jb 5/2, II Sm 3/30. So also with the
verb קָרָא, e.g. וַיִּקְרָא אֱלֹהִים לָאוֹר יוֹם (Gn 1/5);   cf. Gn
1/10. Contrast Gn 26/33, and compare the passive verb
in Gn 2/23. It may also appear in place of the normal
subject of a passive verb, e.g. פֶּן יְבֻלַּע לַמֶּלֶךְ וּלְכָל־הָעָם
(II Sm 17/16).

274   (ix) Norm, expressing mode or manner, and meaning 'according to,' e.g. עֵץ פְּרִי עֹשֶׂה פְּרִי לְמִינוֹ (Gn 1/11);   cf.
Gn 13/17. This is equivalent in meaning to an accusative of manner (cf. § 60), e.g. לְאַט, 'gently' (Is 8/6),
לָבֶטַח, 'securely' (I Kg 5/5), לֶאֱמֶת, 'faithfully' (Is
42/3). With an infinitive לְ expresses the equivalent
of a gerund (cf. § 195). Sometimes this preposition
must be rendered 'as compared with,' e.g. עַד אֲשֶׁר־דַּק
לְעָפָר (Dt 9/21).

275   (x) Degree, with a construct infinitive, meaning 'enough
to . . .' (cf. § 199), e.g. וַיִּתְאַנַּף יְ׳ בָּכֶם לְהַשְׁמִיד אֶתְכֶם
(Dt 9/8);   cf. Dt 9/20, II Sm 13/2.

276   (xi) Introducing, to complete a construct infinitive (cf.

§§ 192 f.), where it is pleonastic, e.g. יוֹדֵעַ לַעֲשׂוֹת בַּזָּהָב (II Ch 2/13), to be contrasted with לֹא־יָדְעוּ עֲשׂוֹת־נְכֹחָה (Am 3/10).

277 (xii) Purpose, e.g. וַיַּעַשׂ אֱלֹהִים . . . אֶת־הַמָּאוֹר הַגָּדֹל לְמֶמְשֶׁלֶת הַיּוֹם (Gn 1/16); cf. Gn 22/7, Ju 20/20. It is espe-cially frequent with the construct infinitive (cf. § 197).

278 (xiii) Product, when an action results in a state or condition, e.g. וְאֶעֶשְׂךָ לְגוֹי גָּדוֹל (Gn 12/2); cf. Ex 7/15, I Sm 15/1, Ex 21/2. It is very common with the verb הָיָה in the meaning 'become' (e.g. Gn 1/14). With a construct infinitive it imparts a gerundive sense (cf. § 196).

279 (xiv) Result, with a construct infinitive (cf. § 198), and occasionally with a substantive, e.g. צֹאן לְטִבְחָה (Je 12/3).

280 (xv) Agent, with passive verbs, e.g. הֲלוֹא נָכְרִיּוֹת נֶחְשַׁבְנוּ לוֹ (Gn 31/15); cf. Ex 12/16.

281 (xvi) Distributive (cf. § 103), e.g. וַתִּפְקְדֶנּוּ לִבְקָרִים לִרְגָעִים תִּבְחָנֶנּוּ (Jb 7/18); cf. I Sm 29/2, I Kg 10/22.

282 (xvii) Assistance or partisanship, meaning 'for,' 'on the side of,' e.g. הֲלָנוּ אַתָּה אִם־לְצָרֵינוּ (Jo 5/13).

283 (xviii) Asseverative, as in Ugaritic, with a substan-tive, e.g. כִּי לַי' מָגִנֵּנוּ וְלִקְדוֹשׁ יִשְׂרָאֵל מַלְכֵּנוּ, 'truly Yahweh is our shield; truly the Holy One of Israel is our king' (Ps 89/19); cf. Jb 13/12.

284 (xix) Obligation, a rare use (mostly late) meaning 'en-cumbent upon' (so עַל, cf. § 294), e.g. הֲלֹא לָכֶם לָדַעַת

אֶת־הַמִּשְׁפָּט (Mi 3/1);   cf. I Sm 23/20, II Ch 13/5.

285   (d) עַל, expressing motion or rest on or above something.
       This was originally a substantive (cf. II Sm 23/1, Gn
       49/25).

286   (i) Locative, to be rendered 'on,' e.g. עַל הָאֲדָמָה (Ex
       20/12);   'over,' 'above,' e.g. עַל־הָאָרֶץ (Gn 1/20; cf.
       Dt 28/23);   'beside,' e.g. עַל־קִיר הַבַּיִת (I Kg 6/5).

287   (ii) Terminative, meaning 'down to/on,' e.g. עַל־הַפְּגָרִים
       (Gn 15/11);   cf. Gn 21/14, Ex 20/26.

288   (iii) Adversative, expressing disadvantage, e.g. מֵתָה
       עָלַי רָחֵל (Gn 48/7);   cf. Nu 11/13, I Sm 21/16, Ps
       142/4;   sometimes to be rendered 'in spite of' (cf.
       § 530), e.g. עַל־דַּעְתְּךָ כִּי־לֹא אֶרְשָׁע (Jb 10/7);   cf. Jb
       34/6, Is 53/9.

289   (iv) Specification, to be rendered 'concerning,' e.g.
       וְעַל הִשָּׁנוֹת הַחֲלוֹם אֶל־פַּרְעֹה פַּעֲמָיִם (Gn 41/32);   cf. Ex
       22/8.

290   (v) Norm, meaning 'in accordance with,' 'on the basis
       of,' e.g. עַל־צִבְאֹתָם (Ex 12/51), עַל כָּל־הַדְּבָרִים הָאֵלֶּה (Ex 24/8),
       עַל הַמִּשְׁפָּטִים, עַל־יֶתֶר, 'abundantly' (Ps 31/24),
       הָאֵלֶּה (Nu 35/24).

291   (vi) Causal, e.g. הִנְּךָ מֵת עַל־הָאִשָּׁה אֲשֶׁר־לָקַחְתָּ and עַל־כֵּן
       (Gn 20/3);   cf. Dt 9/18;   with an infinitive (cf.
       § 534), e.g. וַיִּקְרָא שֵׁם הַמָּקוֹם מַסָּה וּמְרִיבָה עַל־רִיב בְּנֵי
       יִשְׂרָאֵל וְעַל נַסֹּתָם אֶת־י/ (Ex 17/7);   cf. Je 2/35;   or
       with a noun clause (cf. § 533), e.g. וַיִּגְנֹב יַעֲקֹב אֶת־
       לֵב לָבָן הָאֲרַמִּי עַל־בְּלִי הִגִּיד לוֹ כִּי בֹרֵחַ הוּא (Gn 31/20).

54

292   (vii) Addition, e.g. כִּי־יָסַפְנוּ עַל־כָּל־חַטֹּאתֵינוּ רָעָה (I Sm

12/19),   וַיִּקַּח אֶת־מָחֲלַת . . . עַל־נָשָׁיו לוֹ לְאִשָּׁה(Gn 28/9);

cf. Nu 31/8, 28/10.

293   (viii) Accompaniment, e.g. עַל־מְרֹרִים יֹאכְלֻהוּ (Ex 12/8);

cf. Ex 35/22, I Kg 15/20.

294   (ix) Obligation, meaning 'encumbent upon,' e.g. וְעָלַי

דָתַת לְךָ עֲשָׂרָה כֶסֶף וַחֲגֹרָה אֶחָת (II Sm 18/11;   cf. II Kg

18/14);   cf. Pr 7/14, I Kg 4/7.

295   (x) Advantage, meaning 'on behalf of,' 'for the sake

of,' e.g. אֲשֶׁר־נִלְחַם אָבִי עֲלֵיכֶם (Ju 9/17);   cf. II Kg

10/3, Gn 19/17, I Kg 2/18.

296   (xi) Indirect object, a late use (so אֶל, cf. § 300),

e.g. אִם־עַל־הַמֶּלֶךְ טוֹב (Es 1/19);   cf. Ez 7/28.

297   (e) אֶל, expressing motion towards a person or thing. It

is never used with an infinitive or a noun clause.

298   (i) Terminative, meaning 'into,' 'unto,' e.g. וְלֹא־תָבִיא

תוֹעֵבָה אֶל־בֵּיתֶךָ (Dt 7/26);   cf. Gn 6/18;   equivalent

to לְ (cf. § 266).

299   (ii) Directive, meaning 'towards,' e.g. וַתִּשָּׂא אֵשֶׁת־אֲדֹנָיו

אֶת־עֵינֶיהָ אֶל־יוֹסֵף (Gn 39/7);   cf. I Kg 8/29 f., Gn

32/31;   equivalent to לְ (cf. § 267).

300   (iii) Indirect object, e.g. וַיִּקְרָא אֶל־עֲבָדָיו (II Kg

6/11);   cf. Dt 5/1, Gn 20/17, 16/11;   equivalent to

לְ (cf. § 269).

301   (iv) Assistance or partisanship, meaning 'for,' 'on

the side of,' e.g. מִי מִשֶּׁלָּנוּ אֶל־מֶלֶךְ יִשְׂרָאֵל (II Kg

6/11);   cf. Je 15/1, Ezk 36/9;   equivalent to לְ (cf.

§ 282).

302 (v) Advantage, meaning 'for the sake of,' 'on behalf
of,' e.g. וַיָּנֻסוּ אֶל־נַפְשָׁם (II Kg 7/7); cf. I Kg 19/3;
equivalent to עַל (cf. § 295) and לְ (cf. § 271).

303 (vi) Adversative, expressing disadvantage, e.g. וַיָּקָם
קַיִן אֶל־הֶבֶל אָחִיו (Gn 4/8); cf. Nu 32/14, Je 21/13,
33/26; equivalent to עַל (cf. § 288); cf. also לְ
(§ 271).

304 (vii) Accompaniment, e.g. וְלֹא־תֶחֶטְאוּ לַי׳ לֶאֱכֹל אֶל־הַדָּם
(I Sm 14/34); equivalent to עַל (cf. § 293).

305 (viii) Addition, e.g. הוֹסַפְתָּ חָכְמָה וָטוֹב אֶל־הַשְּׁמוּעָה אֲשֶׁר
שָׁמָעְתִּי (I Kg 10/7); equivalent to עַל (cf. § 292).

306 (ix) Specification, meaning 'concerning,' e.g. כִּי־הִתְאַבֵּל
שְׁמוּאֵל אֶל־שָׁאוּל (I Sm 15/35); cf. II Sm 24/16, I Sm
4/19; equivalent to עַל (cf. § 289); cf. also לְ
(§ 273).

307 (x) Norm, meaning 'in accordance with,' 'on the basis
of,' e.g. אֶל־פִּי י׳ (Jo 15/13), אֶל־נָכוֹן, 'assuredly'
(I Sm 23/23); equivalent to עַל (cf. § 290); cf. also
לְ (§ 274).

308 (xi) Locative, meaning 'at,' 'by,' 'near,' e.g. וַיִּשְׁחָטוּהוּ
אֶל־מַעְבְּרוֹת הַיַּרְדֵּן (Ju 12/6); cf. I Kg 13/20; equivalent to עַל (cf. § 286).

(f) עַד

309 (i) Terminative, meaning 'as far as,' e.g. וַיָּבֹאוּ עַד־חָרָן
(Gn 11/31); cf. I Sm 9/9.

310 (ii) Locative, meaning 'near,' 'at,' 'by,' e.g. וַיֶּאֱהַל

עַד־סְדֹם (Gn 13/12);   cf. Ju 4/11, Dt 2/23.

311   (iii) Temporal, meaning 'until,' e.g. עַד הַיּוֹם הַזֶּה (Gn

26/33);   also with a construct infinitive (cf. § 507),

e.g. עַד שׁוּבְךָ אֶל־הָאֲדָמָה (Gn 3/19);   cf. I Kg 18/29 (with

introducing לְ;   cf. § 276);   or a noun clause intro-

duced by אֲשֶׁר (cf. § 501), e.g. וְלֹא־הֶאֱמַנְתִּי לַדְּבָרִים עַד

אֲשֶׁר־בָּאתִי וַתִּרְאֶינָה עֵינַי (I Kg 10/7), or כִּי, e.g. וַיִּצְבֹּר

יוֹסֵף בָּר . . . עַד כִּי־חָדַל לִסְפֹּר (Gn 41/49).   With the

meaning 'by' it occurs in יוּמַת עַד־הַבֹּקֶר (Ju 6/31);   cf.

I Sm 25/22; so also with an infinitive, e.g. עַד־אוֹר

הַבֹּקֶר (II Sm 17/22).   Rarely it has the meaning of

'during,' 'while' (cf. Aramaic עַד), e.g. מָה הַשָּׁלוֹם עַד־

זְנוּנֵי אִיזֶבֶל (II Kg 9/22);   cf. Ju 3/26, I Sm 14/19.

With a negative לֹא עַד־לֹא means 'before,' e.g. עַד־לֹא עָשָׂה

אֶרֶץ וְחוּצוֹת (Pr 8/26;   parallelled by בְּטֶרֶם in v. 25).

312   (iv) Degree, meaning 'up to,' e.g. וְעַד־הַשְּׁלֹשָׁה לֹא־בָא (II Sm

23/19);   cf. I Sm 11/15, I Ch 4/27;   so also with an

infinitive, e.g. עַד־הִשְׁלִכוֹ אֹתָם מֵעַל פָּנָיו (II Kg 24/20).

313   (v) Inclusive, in the construction מִן . . . (וְ)עַד, often

to be rendered 'both . . . and' (cf. § 327), e.g. מִקָּטֹן

וְעַד־גָּדוֹל (I Sm 5/9); cf. Gn 19/4, Ex 9/25;   sometimes

without מִן, e.g. וַיִּתְּנֵהוּ לְדָוִד וּמַדָּיו וְעַד־חַרְבּוֹ וְעַד־קַשְׁתּוֹ

וְעַד־חֲגֹרוֹ (I Sm 18/4);   cf. Lv 11/42, Nu 8/4.

314   (vi) Emphatic, to be rendered 'even,' e.g. לֹא־נִשְׁאַר בָּהֶם

עַד־אֶחָד (Ex 14/28);   cf. II Sm 17/22, Jb 25/5.

   (g) מִן

315   (i) Separative, e.g. כִּי־יִפֹּל הַנֹּפֵל מִמֶּנּוּ (Dt 22/8);   cf.

Jo 10/7, Dt 30/3.

316 (ii) Temporal, e.g. מִיּוֹם דַּעְתִּי אֶתְכֶם (Dt 9/24); cf. I Sm
18/9; hence in the meaning 'after,' e.g. וַיְהִי כְּמִשְׁלֹשׁ
חֳדָשִׁים (Gn 38/24); cf. Ho 6/2, Ps 73/20.

317 (iii) Comparative, with an adjective (cf. § 76), e.g.
מַה־פָּתוֹק מִדְּבַשׁ וּמֶה עַז מֵאֲרִי (Ju 14/18); cf. Ezk 28/3.
It is sometimes followed by an infinitive, e.g. טוֹב
תִּתִּי אֹתָהּ לָךְ מִתִּתִּי אֹתָהּ לְאִישׁ אַחֵר (Gn 29/19).

318 (iv) Absolute comparative (elative), expressing a quality of too high a degree, e.g. הֲיִפָּלֵא מְיִ/ הָבָר (Gn
18/14); cf. Dt 14/24, Nu 11/14; so also with an infinitive, e.g. כִּי־הָיָה רְכוּשָׁם רָב מִשֶּׁבֶת יַחְדָּו (Gn 36/7);
cf. I Kg 8/64.

319 (v) Causal, e.g. הָרִים רָעֲשׁוּ מִמֶּנּוּ . . . וַתִּשָּׂא הָאָרֶץ מִפָּנָיו
(Na 1/5 f.); cf. Ex 2/23; with an infinitive (cf.
§ 534), e.g. לֹא מֵרֻבְּכֶם מִכָּל־הָעַמִּים חָשַׁק י/ בָּכֶם (Dt 7/7);
cf. II Sm 3/11; with a noun clause introduced by אֲשֶׁר
(cf. § 533), e.g. מֵאֲשֶׁר יָקַרְתָּ בְעֵינַי (Is 43/4).

320 (vi) Means, e.g. וְלֹא־יִכָּרֵת כָּל־בָּשָׂר עוֹד מִמֵּי הַמַּבּוּל (Gn
9/11); cf. Jb 7/14. Used rarely also for an agent,
e.g. וְאִשָּׁה גְּרוּשָׁה מֵאִישָׁהּ (Lv 21/7).

321 (vii) Privative, meaning 'deprived of,' 'without,' e.g.
בְּצֵל חֶשְׁבּוֹן עָמְדוּ מִכֹּחַ נָסִים (Je 48/45); cf. I Sm 15/23;
with an infinitive, e.g. וַיִּמְאָסְךָ י/ מִהְיוֹת מֶלֶךְ עַל־יִשְׂרָאֵל
(I Sm 15/26); cf. Lv 26/13; even with a noun clause,
e.g. מִן־יְקוּמוּן (Dt 33/11).

322 (viii) Source, e.g. אִבְצָן מִבֵּית לָחֶם (Ju 12/8); cf. Gn 2/7,
I Sm 24/14, I Kg 2/15.

323 (ix) Relationship: (1) In space, e.g. מִקֶּדֶם לְבֵית־אֵל (Gn

12/8), מִצָּפוֹן לָעִיר (Jo 8/13), מֵעֵבֶר לַיַּרְדֵּן (Nu 32/19);

cf. Dt 5/8. (2) In time, e.g. מִמָּחֳרָת (Gn 19/34), מֵאָז

(II Sm 15/34). (3) Sometimes it is to be rendered

'before,' 'in the sight of' (i.e. from the standpoint

of), e.g. וִהְיִיתֶם נְקִיִּים מֵי/ וּמִיִּשְׂרָאֵל (Nu 32/22), הָאֱנוֹשׁ

שֶׁנּוֹאָה לָאדוֹן מֵאֱלוֹהַּ יִצְדָּק אִם מֵעֹשֵׂהוּ יִטְהַר־גָּבֶר (Jb 4/17),

ואנשים גאוה ומשניהם מעל עשק (Si 10/7); cf. Je 51/5.

324 (x) Partitive, e.g. וַיֵּצְאוּ מִן־הָעָם לִלְקֹט (Ex 16/27), וַיָּבֵא

קַיִן מִפְּרִי הָאֲדָמָה (Gn 4/3); cf. I Kg 18/5.

325 (xi) Emphatic (similar to עַד, cf. § 314), e.g. וְעָשָׂה

מֵאַחַת מֵהֵנָּה, 'if he does any one of them' (Lv 4/2), חַי־

י/, אִם־יִפֹּל מִשַּׂעֲרַת בְּנֵךְ אַרְצָה, 'As Yahweh lives, not even

a hair of your son shall fall to the ground' (II Sm

14/11 = I Sm 14/45).

326 (xii) Explicative, meaning 'consisting of,' e.g. וַיִּקְחוּ

הַבַּרְ־מִי יָקוּם מִפְּנֵי וּמֵהֶם (Gn 6/2), לָהֶם נָשִׁים מִכֹּל אֲשֶׁר בָּחָרוּ

(Je 44/28); cf. Gn 7/22, 9/10, Lv 11/32, I Ch 5/18,

Je 40/7.

327 (xiii) Inclusive, in the construction עַד(!) . . . מִן,

often to be rendered 'both . . . and' (cf. § 313),

e.g. מִנַּעַר וְעַד־זָקֵן (Gn 19/4); cf. I Sm 5/9, Ex 9/25;

occasionally followed by the directive הָ in place of

עַד, e.g. מִכֹּל חֹגֵר חֲגֹרָה וָמָעְלָה (II Kg 3/21).

  (h) עִם

328 (i) Accompaniment, e.g. הוּא וְהָאֲנָשִׁים אֲשֶׁר־עִמּוֹ (Gn 24/54);

cf. Dt 12/23.

59

329 (ii) Locative, meaning 'near,' 'beside,' e.g. וַיֵּשֶׁב יִצְחָק
עִם־בְּאֵר לַחַי רֹאִי (Gn 25/11); cf. Ju 18/3.

330 (iii) Possession, e.g. גַּם־תֶּבֶן גַּם־מִסְפּוֹא רַב עִמָּנוּ (Gn
24/25); cf. Gn 31/32.

331 (iv) Advantage, e.g. וְאֵיטִיבָה עִמָּךְ (Gn 32/10); cf. Gn
24/12, 26/29.

332 (v) Adversative or disadvantage, meaning 'against,' e.g.
אִם־תַּעֲשֵׂה עִמָּנוּ רָעָה (Gn 26/29); cf. Ps 94/16; sometimes
to be rendered 'in spite of,' e.g. וְעִם־זֶה לֶחֶם הַפֶּחָה לֹא
בִקַּשְׁתִּי (Ne 5/18).

333 (vi) Co-ordination, meaning 'and,' 'as well as,' e.g.
עִם־עָרֵיהֶם הֶחֱרִימָם יְהוֹשֻׁעַ (Jo 11/21).

334 (vii) Comparison, e.g. וְנִמְשַׁלְתִּי עִם־יוֹרְדֵי בוֹר (Ps 28/1);
cf. Jb 9/26.

335 (viii) Reciprocal, e.g. וּפְלִשְׁתִּים נֶאֶסְפוּ לְהִלָּחֵם עִם־יִשְׂרָאֵל
(I Sm 13/5); cf. Gn 30/8, 26/28, Jo 22/8.

336 (ix) Assistance, e.g. כִּי־עִם־אֱלֹהִים עָשָׂה הַיּוֹם הַזֶּה (I Sm
14/45); cf. Da 11/39.

337 (x) Consciousness, derived from the expression עִם־לֵבָב,
e.g. וַיְהִי עִם־לְבַב דָּוִד אָבִי לִבְנוֹת בַּיִת (I Kg 8/17; cf.
10/2), כִּי לֹא־כֵן אָנֹכִי עִמָּדִי (Jb 9/35); cf. Jb 10/13,
II Sm 6/22.

(i) אֵת

338 (i) Accompaniment, e.g. וְנָשְׂאוּ אִתָּךְ (Ex 18/22).

339 (ii) Locative, meaning 'near,' 'beside,' e.g. וְהוּא שָׁב
מִן־הַפְּסִילִים אֲשֶׁר אֶת־הַגִּלְגָּל (Ju 3/19); cf. I Kg 9/26.

340 (iii) Possession, e.g. מָה אִתָּנוּ (I Sm 9/7); cf. Gn 27/15,

Ju 17/2.

341   (iv) Advantage, e.g. כְּכֹל אֲשֶׁר עָשָׂה אִתְּכֶם בְּמִצְרַיִם (Dt 1/30);
       cf. Dt 10/21, I Sm 12/7.

342   (v) Adversative or disadvantage, e.g. וְאַתָּה עֹשֶׂה אִתִּי רָעָה
       (Ju 11/27).

343   (vi) Co-ordination, meaning 'and,' 'as well as,' e.g.
       וְהִנְנִי מַשְׁחִיתָם אֶת־הָאָרֶץ (Gn 6/13).

344   (vii) Reciprocal, e.g. וְאִשָּׁפְטָה אִתְּכֶם לִפְנֵי יי (I Sm 12/7);
       cf. Is 53/12.

345   (viii) Assistance, meaning 'by the help of' (rarer
       than עִם, cf. § 336), e.g. קָנִיתִי אִישׁ אֶת־יי (Gn 4/1);
       cf. Jb 26/4, Ju 8/7.

346   (ix) Partisanship, meaning 'for,' 'on the side of,'
       e.g. וַיֹּאמֶר מִי אִתִּי (II Kg 9/32).

347   (x) Consciousness (cf. § 337), e.g. כִּי־פְשָׁעֵינוּ אִתָּנוּ (Is
       59/12); cf. Jb 12/3, Gn 40/14.

348 (j) תַּחַת, actually the bound form of a substantive, often
     employed in the accusative of manner (e.g. Gn 49/25)
     or with the preposition מִן of relationship (cf. § 323,
     e.g. Ex 20/4).

349   (i) Locative, meaning 'under,' e.g. תַּחַת כָּל־הַשָּׁמָיִם (Gn
       7/19), or 'at the base of,' e.g. וַיִּבֶן מִזְבֵּחַ תַּחַת הָהָר
       (Ex 24/4).

350   (ii) Authority or control, e.g. וְיִצְבְּרוּ־בָר תַּחַת יַד־פַּרְעֹה
       (Gn 41/35), וְאִם־לֹא שָׂטִית טֻמְאָה תַּחַת אִישֵׁךְ (Nu 5/19);
       cf. Is 24/5.

351   (iii) Identity of situation, to be rendered 'in one's

61

place,' 'on the spot,' e.g. וְעָמַדְנוּ תַחְתֵּינוּ (I Sm
14/9); cf. II Sm 2/23.

352   (iv) Exchange, meaning 'in place of,' 'instead of,'
        e.g. וַיַּעֲלֵהוּ לְעֹלָה תַּחַת בְּנוֹ (Gn 22/13); cf. I Kg 11/43,
        21/2, Ex 21/23; with a noun clause introduced by
        אֲשֶׁר, e.g. וְנִשְׁאַרְתֶּם בִּמְתֵי מְעָט תַּחַת אֲשֶׁר הֱיִיתֶם כְּכוֹכְבֵי
        הַשָּׁמַיִם לָרֹב (Dt 28/62).

353   (v) Causal, with noun clauses introduced by אֲשֶׁר (cf.
        § 533), e.g. תַּחַת אֲשֶׁר קִנֵּא לֵאלֹהָיו (Nu 25/13); cf. II
        Kg 22/17; or by כִּי, e.g. וְתַחַת כִּי אָהַב אֶת־אֲבֹתֶיךָ (Dt
        4/37).

354   (k) בְּעַד, the bound form of the substantive בַּעַד (Ca 4/1,
        3; 6/7).

355   (i) Locative, meaning 'behind,' e.g. וַיִּסְגְּרוּ בַעֲדָם (Ju
        9/51), or 'through,' e.g. וַתּוֹרִדֵם בַּחֶבֶל בְּעַד הַחַלּוֹן (Jo
        2/15); cf. Ju 5/28.

356   (ii) Advantage, meaning 'on behalf of,' e.g. וְאֶתְפַּלֵּל
        בַּעַדְכֶם אֶל־יְ/ (I Sm 7/5); cf. I Sm 7/9, Ex 32/30.

357   (1) אַחֲרֵי/אַחַר, probably the bound form of a substantive
        meaning 'butt'(?) (II Sm 2/23); with suffixes the
        plural form is always used.

358   (i) Locative, meaning 'behind,' 'after,' e.g. וַיֵּלֶךְ
        יוֹסֵף אַחַר אֶחָיו (Gn 37/17); cf. II Kg 13/2, Dt 11/28,
        I Sm 14/13. It was an easy transition from the
        meaning 'after' to 'in the retinue of,' and thence
        to 'with,' e.g. Ne 3/16-31 (where אַחֲרָיו is parallel-
        led by עַל־יָדוֹ), Dt 23/15, Am 7/15.

359   (ii) Direction, with the meaning 'west of,' e.g. וַיִּנְהַג

הִנֵּה אַחֲרֵי קִרְיַת יְעָרִים (Ex 3/1), אֶת־הַצֹּאן אַחַר הַמִּדְבָּר (Ju

18/12); cf. Jo 8/2, Ezk 41/15, Dt 11/30.

360   (iii) Temporal, meaning 'after,' e.g. אַחַר הַדְּבָרִים הָאֵלֶּה

(Gn 15/1), וְגַם אַחֲרֵי־כֵן (Gn 6/4); cf. Gn 9/28; with

an infinitive (cf. § 505), e.g. אַחֲרֵי הִפָּרֶד־לוֹט מֵעִמּוֹ

(Gn 13/14); cf. I Kg 13/23; with a noun clause

(cf. § 500), e.g. וַיְהִי אַחַר הַדְּבָר / אֶת־הַדְּבָרִים הָאֵלֶּה

(Jb 42/7); cf. I Sm 5/9. This may be introduced by

אֲשֶׁר, e.g. אַחֲרֵי אֲשֶׁר־כָּרְתוּ לָהֶם בְּרִית (Jo 9/16).

361   (iv) Adversative, meaning 'against,' e.g. אַחֲרֶיךָ רֹאשׁ

הֵנִיעָה בַּת יְרוּשָׁלַ͏ִם (II Kg 19/21); cf. I Kg 14/10,

21/21.

362   (v) Norm, meaning 'in accordance with,' 'after the man-

ner of,' e.g. וַיִּסְפֹּר שְׁלֹמֹה כָּל־הָאֲנָשִׁים . . . אַחֲרֵי הַסְּפָר

אֲשֶׁר סְפָרָם דָּוִיד אָבִיו (II Ch 2/16); cf. Is 65/2, Ezk

13/3.

363   (m) יַעַן, also the bound form of an original substantive.

Always in a causal sense: rarely with substantives,

e.g. יַעַן כָּל־תּוֹעֲבֹתָיִךְ (Ezk 5/9); with an infinitive (cf.

§ 534), e.g. יַעַן הִתְמַכֶּרְךָ לַעֲשׂוֹת הָרַע (I Kg 21/20); with

a noun clause (cf. § 533), e.g. יַעַן לֹא־הֶאֱמַנְתֶּם בִּי (Nu

20/12), which may be introduced by אֲשֶׁר (e.g. Gn 22/16)

or כִּי (e.g. Nu 11/20).

364   (n) לְמַעַן, a compound formed of a preposition and a sub-

stantive.

365   (i) Advantage, meaning 'for the sake of,' e.g. וְלֹא־תִשָּׂא

לַמָּקוֹם לְמַעַן חֲמִשִּׁים הַצַּדִּיקִם אֲשֶׁר בְּקִרְבָּהּ (Gn 18/24);   cf.
Dt 30/6.

366 (ii) Causal, meaning 'on account of,' e.g. יִתְעַבֵּר יְ /
בִּי לְמַעַנְכֶם (Dt 3/26);   cf. I Kg 11/39.

367 (iii) Purpose (cf. § 197), with an infinitive (cf.
§ 519), e.g. וְיֵהוּא עָשָׂה בְעָקְבָּה לְמַעַן הַאֲבִיד אֶת־עֹבְדֵי הַבַּעַל
(II Kg 10/19);   cf. Gn 37/22;   with a noun clause
and the imperfect aspect (cf. § 520), e.g. לְמַעַן
יִיטַב־לִי בַעֲבוּרֵךְ (Gn 12/13), often introduced by אֲשֶׁר,
e.g. לְמַעַן אֲשֶׁר אֶרְאֶה (II Sm 13/5);   in the negative
with לֹא, e.g. לְמַעַן אֲשֶׁר לֹא־יִקְרַב אִישׁ זָר (Nu 17/5).

368 (iv) Result, a rare use (cf. §§ 198,525), with an infinitive, e.g. וַיְקַטְּרוּ לֵאלֹהִים אֲחֵרִים לְמַעַן הַכְעִיסֵנִי (II
Kg 22/17).

369 (o) לִפְנֵי, a compound formed of a preposition and a substantive in the bound form.

370 (i) Locative, meaning 'before,' 'in front of,' e.g.
וְאַבְרָהָם עוֹדֶנּוּ עֹמֵד לִפְנֵי יְ / (Gn 18/22).

371 (ii) Temporal, meaning 'before,' e.g. שְׁנָתַיִם לִפְנֵי הָרַעַשׁ
(Am 1/1);   with an infinitive (cf. § 506), e.g. לִפְנֵי
שַׁחֵת יְ / אֶת־סְדֹם וְאֶת־עֲמֹרָה (Gn 13/10).

372 (iii) Mental, meaning 'in the sight of,' e.g. כִּי־אֹתְךָ
רָאִיתִי צַדִּיק לְפָנַי (Gn 7/1);   cf. I Sm 20/1, II Kg 5/1.

373 (iv) Comparison, meaning 'like' (a rare use), e.g. אַל־
תִּתֵּן אֶת־אֲמָתְךָ לִפְנֵי בַּת־בְּלִיָּעַל (I Sm 1/16);   cf. Jb 3/24,
4/19.

374 (p) מִפְּנֵי, a compound formed of a preposition and the

64

bound form of a substantive.

375   (i) Locative, meaning 'from (before),' e.g. וַיִּסַּע עַמּוּד
הֶעָנָן מִפְּנֵיהֶם (Ex 14/19).

376   (ii) Causal, e.g. כִּי־מָלְאָה הָאָרֶץ חָמָס מִפְּנֵיהֶם (Gn 6/13);
cf. Ex 3/7; with a noun clause introduced by אֲשֶׁר
(cf. § 533), e.g. וְהַר סִינַי עָשַׁן כֻּלּוֹ מִפְּנֵי אֲשֶׁר יָרַד עָלָיו
/' בָּאֵשׁ (Ex 19/18).

2. Adverbs

377 Hebrew possesses very few adverbs. These are normally
replaced by substantives in the accusative of manner (cf.
§ 60) or with the preposition בְּ of norm (cf. § 252), e.g.
טֶרֶם and בְּטֶרֶם, the similarly employed prepositions לְ (cf.
§ 274) or עַל (cf. § 290), or the first element in verbal
co-ordination (cf. § 223). Substantives with adverbial
endings are often used, e.g. שִׁלְשׁוֹם, יוֹמָם, רֵיקָם, חִנָּם, אָמְנָם,
פִּתְאֹם. For negative adverbs see §§ 394 ff. A few adverbs
of manner are here discussed.

(a) גַּם

378 (i) Addition, meaning 'also,' either with a following
word, e.g. וַתִּתֵּן גַּם־לְאִישָׁהּ עִמָּהּ (Gn 3/6); cf. Gn 4/4,
27/34; or with a clause, e.g. גַּם כִּי־אָמַר אֵלַי (Ru 2/21).
Hence גַּם(וֹ) . . . גַּם, 'both . . . and,' e.g. גַּם־אֲנַחְנוּ
גַּם אֲשֶׁר־נִמְצָא הַגָּבִיעַ בְּיָדוֹ (Gn 44/16); cf. I Sm 20/27
(negative).

379 (ii) Emphatic, meaning 'even,' 'just,' like Greek καί,
e.g. וְהָיָה אִם־לֹא יַאֲמִינוּ גַּם לִשְׁנֵי הָאֹתוֹת הָאֵלֶּה (Ex 4/9),

65

וְאָבִי רְאֵה גַּם רְאֵה אֶת־כְּנַף מְעִילְךָ בְּיָדִי (I Sm 24/12);
cf. Nu 22/33, Gn 20/4, 46/4.

380   (iii) Rhetorical, e.g. גַּם־בָּרוּךְ יִהְיֶה, 'Yes, and he
      shall be blessed!' (Gn 27/33), מַדּוּעַ רְשָׁעִים יִחְיוּ עָתְקוּ
      גַּם־גָּבְרוּ חָיִל (Jb 21/7);   cf. Is 13/3, Je 6/15.

381   (iv) Correlative, meaning 'on one's part,' e.g. גַּם־יְ/
      הֶעֱבִיר חַטָּאתְךָ (II Sm 12/13);   cf. I Sm 1/28.

382   (v) Concessive, meaning 'although,' 'even though' (cf.
      § 529), e.g. בְּחָנוּנִי גַּם־רָאוּ פָעֳלִי (Ps 95/9);   so also
      with כִּי, e.g. גַּם כִּי־תַרְבּוּ תְפִלָּה אֵינֶנִּי שֹׁמֵעַ (Is 1/15);
      cf. § 448.

383   (b) אַף, rare in prose, but common in poetry.

384   (i) Addition, meaning 'also,' with a following word,
      e.g. אַף־אֲנִי בַּחֲלוֹמִי (Gn 40/16);   cf. I Sm 2/7;   with
      a clause, e.g. אַף לֹא אֶל־אֶרֶץ זָבַת חָלָב וּדְבַשׁ הֲבִיאֹתָנוּ
      (Nu 16/14).

385   (ii) Emphatic, e.g. אַף־עַל־זֶה פָּקַחְתָּ עֵינֶךָ (Jb 14/3);   cf.
      Jb 15/4, Gn 18/13;   with a clause, e.g. אַף כִּי־אָמַר
      אֱלֹהִים (Gn 3/1).   In a question, this indicates some-
      thing contrary to expectation, e.g. הַאַף תָּפֵר מִשְׁפָּטִי
      (Jb 40/8);   cf. Jb 34/17.

386   (iii) Rhetorical, in poetry, e.g. אַף בַּל־נִטָּעוּ אַף בַּל־
      זֹרָעוּ אַף בַּל־שֹׁרֵשׁ בָּאָרֶץ גִּזְעָם (Is 40/24), יִתְרֹעֲעוּ אַף־יָשִׁירוּ
      (Ps 65/14);   cf. Is 42/13, Ps 16/6, Pr 23/28.

387   (iv) A fortiori, meaning 'how much more/less,' fol-
      lowed by כִּי, e.g. הֵן צַדִּיק בָּאָרֶץ יְשֻׁלָּם אַף כִּי־רָשָׁע וְחוֹטֵא
      (Pr 11/31);   cf. Jb 9/14, 15/16, I Kg 8/27, I Sm

14/30. This כִּי is omitted when a second one follows,

e.g. וְאַף כִּי־אָמַר אֵלֶיךָ רְחַץ וּטְהָר (II Kg 5/13); cf. I Sm

23/3, II Sm 4/11.

(c) אַךְ

388 (i) Restrictive, meaning 'only,' with a following word,

e.g. אַל־נָא יִחַר לַאדֹנָי וַאֲדַבְּרָה אַךְ־הַפַּעַם (Gn 18/32); cf.

I Sm 18/8, Je 16/19; with a clause (cf. § 558), e.g.

אַךְ־בָּשָׂר בְּנַפְשׁוֹ דָמוֹ לֹא תֹאכֵלוּ (Gn 9/4); cf. I Sm 18/17,

I Kg 17/13.

389 (ii) Asseverative, meaning 'surely (i.e. nothing else

than),' e.g. אַךְ טָרֹף טֹרָף (Gn 44/28); cf. I Sm 16/6.

(d) רַק

390 (i) Restrictive, meaning 'only,' with a following word,

e.g. רַק הַכִּסֵּא אֶגְדַּל מִמֶּךָ (Gn 41/40); cf. Ex 10/17; with

a clause (cf. § 559), e.g. רַק בַּבָּמוֹת הוּא מְזַבֵּחַ וּמַקְטִיר

(I Kg 3/3); cf. Gn 24/8. It is used redundantly with

אַךְ in הֲרַק אַךְ־בְּמֹשֶׁה דִּבֶּר י׳ (Nu 12/2).

391 (ii) Asseverative, meaning 'nothing but,' 'only,' 'sure-

ly,' e.g. וְכָל־יֵצֶר מַחְשְׁבֹת לִבּוֹ רַק רַע כָּל־הַיּוֹם (Gn 6/5);

cf. Gn 26/29; with a clause, e.g. רַק־שְׂנֵאתַנִי וְלֹא

אֲהֵבְתָּנִי (Ju 14/16).

392 (iii) Exceptive or limitative, after a negative, with

the meaning 'except,' e.g. אֵין בָּאָרוֹן רַק שְׁנֵי לֻחוֹת הָאֲבָנִים

(I Kg 8/9); cf. II Kg 17/18.

393 (iv) Emphatic, with conditional אִם, meaning 'if . . .

just,' 'if only,' e.g. רַק אִם־שָׁמוֹעַ תִּשְׁמַע בְּקוֹל י׳ אֱלֹהֶיךָ

(Dt 15/5); cf. I Kg 8/25.

67

3. Negatives

394 Double negatives, when they occur, merely add emphasis,

e.g. הֲמִבְּלִי אֵין־אֱלֹהִים בְּיִשְׂרָאֵל (II Kg 1/3, 6, 16);   cf. Ex

14/11, Zp 2/2.

(a) לֹא

395 (i) Objective denial of a fact, like Greek οὐ. Used

with both perfect and imperfect aspects, e.g. וְאֶל־קַיִן

לֹא־אֹסִף לְקַלֵּל עוֹד אֶת־הָאֲדָמָה (Gn 4/5), וְאֶל־מִנְחָתוֹ לֹא שָׁעָה

(Gn 8/21).

396 (ii) Prohibition, with the imperfect aspect (cf. § 173),

e.g. לֹא תֹאכַל מִמֶּנּוּ (Gn 2/17).

397 (iii) With the gerundive use of the construct infinitive

(cf. § 196), e.g. וְלֹא לְהִתְיַחֵשׂ לַבְּכֹרָה (I Ch 5/1);   cf.

Am 6/10, I Ch 15/2, Ju 1/19.

398 (iv) Elliptic (cf. § 590), e.g. וַיֹּאמֶר לֹא (Ju 12/5);   cf.

Gn 18/15.

399 (v) With nominal or adverbial predicates: (1) adjec-

tives, e.g. לֹא־טוֹב הֱיוֹת הָאָדָם לְבַדּוֹ (Gn 2/18);   cf. Ex

18/17;   (2) passive participles, e.g. אֲשֶׁר לֹא כָתוּב בְּסֵפֶר

הַתּוֹרָה הַזֹּאת (Dt 28/61);   cf. II Sm 3/34;   (3) substan-

tives, e.g. הֲלֹא יִרְאָתְךָ כִּסְלָתֶךָ (Jb 4/6);   cf. Jb 9/32,

Ex 4/10, Nu 23/19;   (4) prepositional phrases, e.g.

לֹא בָאֵשׁ י׳ (I Kg 19/12);   cf. I Kg 19/11, Jb 28/14.

400 (vi) Privative, e.g. הוּא־בֵן לֹא חָכָם (Ho 13/13);   cf.

Ps 36/5, Je 2/2, Is 10/15;   also with the preposi-

tion בְּ (cf. § 252), 'without,' e.g. הוֹי בֹּנֶה בֵיתוֹ בְּלֹא־

צֶדֶק (Je 22/13);   cf. Jb 8/11, Nu 35/23.

68

(b) אַל

401   (i) Subjective denial of a wish, like Greek μή. Used
with the precative (cf. § 184), e.g. אַל־אֶרְאֶה בְּמוֹת
הַיָּלֶד (Gn 21/16).

402   (ii) Vetitive, with the precative (cf. § 186), e.g.
אַל־תִּירָא אַבְרָם (Gn 15/1).

403   (iii) Elliptic (cf. § 591), e.g. וַיֹּאמֶר לוֹ מֶלֶךְ יִשְׂרָאֵל אַל
(II Kg 3/13); cf. Ru 1/13.

404   (iv) In an elliptic statement with the לְ of obligation
(cf. § 284) and a modal sense: אַל לַמְלָכִים שְׁתוֹ־יָיִן
(Pr 31/4).

405   (v) As a substantive, occurring in only one poetic
passage: וְיָשֵׂם לְאַל מִלָּתִי (Jb 24/25).

406 (c) אַיִן, properly a substantive (cf. Is 40/17, 23) like
יֵשׁ (cf. § 476).

407   (i) In a bound structure with a following genitive
e.g. וְהִנֵּה אֵין־יוֹסֵף בַּבּוֹר (Gn 37/29); especially with
the subjects of participles, e.g. אֵינֶנִּי נֹתֵן לָכֶם תֶּבֶן
(Ex 5/10); cf. Gn 39/23.

408   (ii) In apposition to a substantive which usually precedes, e.g. וְאָדָם אַיִן לַעֲבֹד אֶת־הָאֲדָמָה (Gn 2/5); cf.
II Kg 19/3.

409   (iii) Elliptic, e.g. וַיַּעַבְרוּ בְאֶרֶץ־שַׁעֲלִים וָאָיִן (I Sm 9/4);
cf. Ex 17/7.

410   (iv) With the gerundive use of the construct infinitive (cf. § 196), with the meaning 'it is not possible to . . .' (mostly late), e.g. וְאֵין עִמָּהּ לְהִתְיַצֵּב

(II Ch 20/6);   cf. Es 4/2, Ez 9/15. This construction may be accompanied by the לְ of obligation (cf.
§ 284), e.g. וְאֵין־לָנוּ אִישׁ לְהָמִית בְּיִשְׂרָאֵל (II Sm 21/4).

411   (v) Privative, with בְּ (cf. § 252), meaning 'without,'
       e.g. הוּא יָמוּת בְּאֵין מוּסָר (Pr 5/23), or לְ (cf. § 274),
       e.g. וַעֲצֵי אֲרָזִים לְאֵין מִסְפָּר (I Ch 22/4).

412   (d) בַּל, only in poetry.

413   (i) Objective denial (like לֹא; cf. § 395), with both
       perfect and imperfect aspects, e.g. אַף בַּל־נִטָּעוּ אַף
       בַּל־זֹרָעוּ אַף בַּל־שֹׁרֵשׁ בָּאָרֶץ גִּזְעָם אָמַר בְּלִבּוֹ בַּל־ (Is 40/24),
       אֶמּוֹט (Ps 10/6);   cf. Ps 147/20.

414   (ii) With nominal or adverbial predicates (like לֹא;
       cf. § 399):   (1) adjectives, e.g. הַכֵּר־פָּנִים בְּמִשְׁפָּט
       בַּל־טוֹב (Pr 24/23);   (2) prepositional phrases, e.g.
       וְלִבּוֹ בַּל־עִמָּךְ (Pr 23/7).

415   (iii) Subjective denial (like אַל;   cf. § 401), with
       the precative, e.g. וּבַל־אֶלְחַם בְּמַנְעַמֵּיהֶם (Ps 141/4).

416   (iv) With a construct infinitive (like לְבִלְתִּי;   cf.
       § 423), only in בַּל קְרֹב אֵלֶיךָ (Ps 32/9).

417   (e) בְּלִי, mostly confined to poetry.

418   (i) Objective denial (like לֹא;   cf. § 395), with both
       perfect and imperfect aspects, e.g. עַל־בְּלִי הִגִּיד לוֹ
       אָסַף בְּלִי יָבוֹא (Is 32/10);   cf. כִּי בֹרֵחַ הוּא (Gn 31/20),
       Dt 28/55, Is 14/6.

419   (ii) With nominal predicates (like לֹא;   cf. § 399),
       either adjectives, e.g. בְּלִי מָשִׁיחַ בַּשָּׁמֶן (II Sm 1/21),
       or participles, e.g. בְּלִי נִשְׁמָע קוֹלָם (Ps 19/4).

70

420   (iii) Privative (like לֹא; cf. § 400), e.g. יִשְׂגֶּה־אָחוּ
       בְּלִי־מָיִם (Jb 8/11); so with an infinitive, e.g. מִבְּלִי
       יְכֹלֶת י' לְַהֲבִיאָם אֶל־הָאָרֶץ (Dt 9/28). Often with the
       prepositions בְּ (cf. § 252) or לְ (cf. § 274), e.g.
       בִּבְלִי־דַעַת (Dt 4/42), לִבְלִי־חֹק (Is 5/14).

    (f) בִּלְתִּי

421   (i) Privative (like לֹא; cf. § 400), e.g. מַכַּת בִּלְתִּי סָרָה
       (Is 14/6), בִּלְתִּי טָהוֹר הוּא (I Sm 20/26).

422   (ii) Limitative, usually after a negative, meaning 'ex-
       cept,' e.g. זֹבֵחַ לָאלֹהִים יָחֳרָם בִּלְתִּי לַי' לְבַדּוֹ (Ex 22/19);
       cf. I Sm 2/2; sometimes also with pleonastic אִם (cf.
       § 457), e.g. אֵין זֹאת בִּלְתִּי אִם־חֶרֶב גִּדְעוֹן (Ju 7/14).
       It may occur with a clause (cf. § 555), e.g. לֹא־תִרְאוּ
       פָנַי בִּלְתִּי אֲחִיכֶם אִתְּכֶם (Gn 43/3), sometimes with pleo-
       nastic אִם, e.g. הֲיֵלְכוּ שְׁנַיִם יַחְדָּו בִּלְתִּי אִם־נוֹעָדוּ (Am
       3/3; cf. v. 4).

423   (iii) To negate construct infinitives, usually with לְ,
       e.g. צִוִּיתִיךָ לְבִלְתִּי אֲכָל־מִמֶּנּוּ (Gn 3/11).

424   (iv) With the preposition לְ before a clause to express
       negative purpose, e.g. לְבִלְתִּי תֶחֱטָאוּ (Ex 20/20); cf.
       II Sm 14/14; cf. §§ 197, 523.

425 (g) אֶפֶס, properly a substantive (cf. Is 34/12, 41/12),
       employed commonly as a poetic synonym of אַיִן.

426   (i) Privative, with a substantive, e.g. עַד אֶפֶס מָקוֹם
       (Is 5/8); cf. II Sm 9/3 (parallel to יֵשׁ in v. 1),
       II Kg 14/26; also with בְּ (cf. § 252), meaning 'with-
       out,' e.g. וַיִּכְלוּ בְּאֶפֶס תִּקְוָה (Jb 7/6); cf. Pr 14/28.

71

427   (ii) Restrictive, meaning 'however,' 'only,' e.g. וְאֶפֶס

אֶת־הַדָּבָר אֲשֶׁר־אֲדַבֵּר אֵלֶיךָ אֹתוֹ תְדַבֵּר (Nu 22/35); or 'yet,'

'nevertheless,' with a noun clause introduced by כִּי

(cf. § 557), e.g. אֶפֶס כִּי לֹא תִהְיֶה תִּפְאַרְתְּךָ עַל־הַדֶּרֶךְ (Ju

4/9).

428   (h) מָה, used occasionally like Arabic mā (cf. § 128),

e.g. מַה־תָּעִירוּ וּמַה־תְּעֹרְרוּ אֶת־הָאַהֲבָה (Ca 8/4; contrast

2/7); cf. Jb 31/1.

4. Conjunctions

429   There are relatively few conjunctions in Hebrew, and
they are frequently replaced by prepositions before
noun clauses.

(a) וְ

430   (i) Co-ordinative, meaning 'and,' e.g. וְלַחֹשֶׁךְ קָרָא לָיְלָה
(Gn 1/5); cf. Gn 10/2.

431   (ii) Disjunctive, expressing a contrast, e.g. טוֹב וָרָע
(Gn 2/17), יוֹם וָלַיְלָה (Gn 8/22).

432   (iii) Adversative, meaning 'but,' e.g. וְנֹחַ מָצָא חֵן
בְּעֵינֵי יְ׳ (Gn 6/8); cf. I Kg 2/26.

433   (iv) Alternative, meaning 'or,' e.g. אַתָּה וּבִנְךָ־וּבִתֶּךָ
עַבְדְּךָ וַאֲמָתְךָ (Ex 20/10); cf. Ex 21/16. However, in
such expressions as שְׁנַיִם שְׁלֹשָׁה סָרִיסִים, 'two or three
eunuchs' (II Kg 9/32), the conjunction is not used.

434   (v) Explicative, to be rendered 'even,' e.g. וְהֶבֶל הֵבִיא
גַם־הוּא מִבְּכֹרוֹת צֹאנוֹ וּמֵחֶלְבֵהֶן (Gn 4/4).

435 (vi) Pleonastic, where it is merely stylistic, as in

Ugaritic, Arabic and Ethiopic, e.g. וַתָּשֶׁב תָּמָר וְשֹׁמֵמָה (II

Sm 13/20), עֶבֶד אָבִיךָ וַאֲנִי מֵאָז וְעַתָּה וַאֲנִי עַבְדֶּךָ (II Sm

15/34); cf. Am 4/10, Jb 4/6.

436 (vii) Accompaniment, meaning 'with,' e.g. וַיָּשִׂמוּ אֶת־אֲרוֹן

יְ אֶל־הָעֲגָלָה וְאֵת הָאַרְגַּז וְאֵת עַכְבְּרֵי הַזָּהָב וְאֵת צַלְמֵי טְחֹרֵיהֶם

(I Sm 6/11); cf. I Sm 25/42, II Sm 12/30; so with

circumstantial clauses (cf. § 494).

437 (viii) Comparative, only in poetry, e.g. הֲלֹא־אֹזֶן מִלִּין

תִּבְחָן וְחֵךְ אֹכֶל יִטְעַם־לוֹ (Jb 12/11); cf. Jb 5/7, 16/21,

Pr 25/25.

438 (ix) Emphatic, meaning 'and specially,' e.g. הַרְבָּה אַרְבֶּה

עִצְּבוֹנֵךְ וְהֵרֹנֵךְ (Gn 3/16); cf. I Kg 11/1.

439 (x) Sarcastic, e.g. וְהִנֵּה יְ עֹשֶׂה אֲרֻבּוֹת בַּשָּׁמַיִם הֲיִהְיֶה כַּדָּבָר

הַזֶּה (II Kg 7/19), וּמִי אֲבִיהֶם (I Sm 10/12); cf. II Sm

18/11, Ju 14/16.

440 (xi) Resumptive, introducing an apodosis, etc., e.g.

יַעַן מָאַסְתָּ אֶת־ (Gn 3/5), בְּיוֹם אֲכָלְכֶם מִמֶּנּוּ וְנִפְקְחוּ עֵינֵיכֶם

הַדְּבַר יְ וַיִּמְאָסְךָ מִמֶּלֶךְ (I Sm 15/23); cf. Gn 18/26, 32/19.

441 (xii) Adjunctive, meaning 'also,' e.g. וְשַׁאֲלִי־לוֹ אֶת־

הַמְּלוּכָה, 'Ask for him the kingdom also!' (I Kg 2/22);

cf. Nu 34/6.

442 (xiii) Distributive (cf. § 101), e.g. עִיר וָעִיר (Ez

10/14); cf. Dt 32/7, I Ch 26/13.

(b) אוֹ

443 Alternative, with substantives, e.g. אִם־עֶבֶד יִגַּח הַשּׁוֹר אוֹ

אָמָה (Ex 21/32), or clauses, e.g. אוֹ־בֵן יִגָּח אוֹ־בַת יִגָּח

73

(Ex 21/31).

(c) כִּי

444 (i) Causal (cf. § 532), e.g. כִּי עָשִׂיתָ זֹּאת אָרוּר אַתָּה (Gn 3/14); cf. Gn 6/12 f.

445 (ii) Temporal (cf. § 496), meaning 'when,' only in ver- bal clauses, e.g. וַיְהִי כִּי־הֵחֵל הָאָדָם לָרֹב (Gn 6/1); cf. Ju 12/5.

446 (iii) Conditional, in real conditions (cf. § 514), e.g. כִּי־תִמְצָא אִישׁ לֹא תְבָרְכֶנּוּ (II Kg 4/29); cf. II Sm 19/8, II Kg 18/22. There is one unusual example in an un- real condition (cf. § 516): כִּי אָמַרְתִּי יֶשׁ־לִי תִקְוָה (Ru 1/12.

447 (iv) Adversative, after a negative (cf. § 553), e.g. לֹא־ תִקְרָא אֶת־שְׁמָהּ שָׂרָי כִּי שָׂרָה שְׁמָהּ (Gn 17/15); cf. I Kg 21/15; it is more common with pleonastic אִם (cf. § 457), e.g. לֹא יַעֲקֹב יֵאָמֵר עוֹד שִׁמְךָ כִּי אִם־יִשְׂרָאֵל (Gn 32/29).

448 (v) Concessive, meaning 'though' (cf. § 529), e.g. כִּי־ תַגְבִּיהַּ כַּנֶּשֶׁר קִנֶּךָ מִשָּׁם אוֹרִידְךָ (Je 49/16); cf. Ps 37/24.

449 (vi) Asseverative, originally in oaths, e.g. חֵי פַרְעֹה כִּי מְרַגְּלִים אַתֶּם (Gn 42/16); cf. I Sm 14/44, sometimes with pleonastic אִם (cf. § 457), e.g. חַי־יְ׳ כִּי־אִם־רַצְתִּי אַחֲרָיו (II Kg 5/20); hence meaning 'truly,' 'indeed,' e.g. לוּלֵא הִתְמַהְמָהְנוּ כִּי־עַתָּה שַׁבְנוּ זֶה פַעֲמָיִם (Gn 43/10); cf. Ps 37/20, Jb 5/2, 14/7.

450 (vii) Resultative (cf. § 526), e.g. הֲכַף זֶבַח וְצַלְמֻנָּע עַתָּה בְיָדְךָ כִּי־נִתֵּן לִצְבָאֲךָ לָחֶם (Ju 8/6); cf. Jb 38/20, II Kg 18/34, Je 2/5.

451   (viii) Nominalizing, introducing noun clauses like Greek

ὅτι, e.g. וַיַּרְא אֱלֹהִים כִּי־טוֹב (Gn 1/10); cf. Gn 22/12;

sometimes after the prepositions תַּחַת, עֵקֶב, עַל, עַד,

יַעַן. Such a clause may occasionally follow the inter-

rogative particle thus, הֲ(לֹא) כִי, with the meaning 'is

it (not) a fact that?' (cf. § 487), e.g. הֲכִי יֶשׁ־עוֹד

אֲשֶׁר נוֹתַר לְבֵית שָׁאוּל (II Sm 9/1); cf. Jb 6/22; הֲלוֹא

כִּי אָנֹכִי צִוִּיתִי אֶתְכֶם (II Sm 13/28); cf. I Sm 10/1.

452   (ix) Recitative, introducing direct speech like Greek

ὅτι, e.g. וַיֹּאמֶר חֲזָהאֵל כִּי מָה עַבְדְּךָ הַכֶּלֶב (II Kg 8/13);

cf. I Kg 21/6, Ex 3/12.

     (d) אִם

453   (i) Conditional,in real conditions (cf. § 514), e.g.

אִם־אֶמְצָא בִסְדֹם חֲמִשִּׁים צַדִּיקִם בְּתוֹךְ הָעִיר וְנָשָׂאתִי לְכָל־הַמָּקוֹם

בַּעֲבוּרָם (Gn 18/26); cf. Gn 31/8. Perhaps, as an ex-

ception, in two passages to introduce an unreal con-

dition: אִם־הִכִּיתֶם כָּל־חֵיל כַּשְׂדִּים . . . יָקוּמוּ (Je 37/10)

and Ps 50/12; cf. § 516.

454   (ii) Concessive (cf. § 528), e.g. אִם־יַעֲמֹד מֹשֶׁה וּשְׁמוּאֵל

לְפָנַי אֵין נַפְשִׁי אֶל־הָעָם הַזֶּה (Je 15/1); cf. Am 9/2-4.

455   (iii) Alternative, in interrogative clauses (cf. § 543),

e.g. הֲלָנוּ אַתָּה אִם־לְצָרֵינוּ (Jo 5/13); cf. II Sm 24/13.

45,6 (iv) Privative, expressing a negative after an oath form-

ula (כֹּה־יַעֲשֶׂה אֱלֹהִים וְכֹה יֹסִף) whether expressed or im-

plied, e.g. חַיָּה וְחֵי נַפְשֶׁךָ אִם־אֶעֱשֶׂה אֶת־הַדָּבָר הַזֶּה (II Sm

11/11); cf. I Sm 17/55, II Kg 3/14. The affirmative

is expressed with לֹא, e.g. אִם־לֹא אֶת־דְּמֵי נָבוֹת וְאֶת־דְּמֵי

75

בָּנָיו רָאִיתִי אֶמֶשׁ (II Kg 9/26);   cf. Jb 1/11.

457   (v) Pleonastic, after עַד (introducing an element of
      doubt) with a noun clause, e.g. עַד אִם־כִּלּוּ אֵת כָּל־הַקָּצִיר
      (Ru 2/21);   cf. Gn 24/19;   sometimes with the particle
      אֲשֶׁר, e.g. עַד וְאֲשֶׁר אִם־הֲבִיאֻם אֶל־מְקוֹמָם (Nu 32/17);   cf.
      Gn 28/15;   after כִּי when adversative or asseverative
      (cf. §§ 447, 449) and after בִּלְתִּי (cf. § 422).

458   (vi) Optative (cf. § 549), rarely in place of לוּ, e.g.
      אִם־תִּקְטֹל אֱלוֹהַּ רָשָׁע (Ps 139/19);   cf. Pr 24/11.

   (e) לוּ

459   (i) Conditional, to introduce unreal conditions (cf.
      § 515), whether in the past (with the perfect aspect),
      e.g. לוּ חָפֵץ ⁄ יְהוָה לַהֲמִיתֵנוּ לֹא־לָקַח מִיָּדֵנוּ עֹלָה וּמִנְחָה (Ju
      13/23);   the present (with a participle), e.g. וְלֹא
      אָנֹכִי שֹׁקֵל עַל־כַּפַּי אֶלֶף כֶּסֶף לֹא־אֶשְׁלַח יָדִי אֶל־בֶּן־הַמֶּלֶךְ (II Sm
      18/12);   or the future (with the imperfect aspect),
      e.g. לוּ־חַיָּה רָעָה אַעֲבִיר בָּאָרֶץ וְשִׁכְּלָתָּה וְהָיְתָה שְׁמָמָה מִבְּלִי
      עוֹבֵר מִפְּנֵי הַחַיָּה (Ezk 14/15).   The negative is expressed
      by לוּלֵא/לוּלֵי, e.g. לוּלֵא חֲרַשְׁתֶּם בְּעֶגְלָתִי לֹא מְצָאתֶם חִידָתִי
      (Ju 14/18);   cf. II Kg 3/14.

460   (ii) Optative (cf. § 547), either in the past (with the
      perfect aspect), e.g. לוּ־מַתְנוּ בְּאֶרֶץ מִצְרַיִם (Nu 14/2);
      or in the future (with the imperfect aspect), e.g. לוּ
      יִשְׁמָעֵאל יִחְיֶה לְפָנֶיךָ (Gn 17/18);   or even with the preca-
      tive mood, e.g. לוּ יְהִי כִדְבָרֶךָ (Gn 30/34).

   (f) פֶּן

461   Before a clause this particle expresses fear or pre-

76

caution, and is to be rendered 'else,' 'lest,' e.g. וְלֹא
תִגְעוּ בּוֹ פֶּן־תְּמֻתוּן (Gn 3/3); cf. Gn 24/6, 32/12. Often
it is used elliptically (cf. § 587), when it means 'be-
ware lest,' e.g. פֶּן־יַסִּית אֶתְכֶם חִזְקִיָּהוּ (Is 36/18); cf.
Dt 29/17.

5. Relative Particles

(a) The Particle אֲשֶׁר

462   By the tenth century B.C., Hebrew (and Moabite) had
abandoned the use of the true relative pronoun (cf.
§ 129), and had substituted for it a particle of relationship אֲשֶׁר, which was derived from an obsolete substantive meaning 'place.' Such a procedure is semanti-
cally akin to the use of wo in colloquial German or ποῦ
in modern Greek as the equivalent of a relative pronoun.
The particle was then employed as a 'gap-word,' to be
resumed by a later element in the clause such as a
pronominal suffix, etc.

463   (i) Relative, e.g. אֲנִי יוֹסֵף אֲחִיכֶם אֲשֶׁר־מְכַרְתֶּם אֹתִי מִצְרָיְמָה
       (Gn 45/4); cf. Ex 3/5, Dt 11/10, Nu 10/29. Sometimes
       it is used without antecedent, e.g. יָדַעְתִּי אֵת אֲשֶׁר־תְּבָרֵךְ
       מְבֹרָךְ וַאֲשֶׁר תָּאֹר יוּאָר (Nu 22/6); cf. Ju 1/12.

464   (ii) Nominalizing, used like כִּי (cf. § 451) and Greek
       ὅτι to introduce noun clauses, e.g. וַיִּרָא שָׁאוּל אֲשֶׁר־הוּא
       מַשְׂכִּיל מְאֹד (I Sm 18/15); cf. Dt 9/7. This is espe-
       cially frequent after prepositions.

465   (iii) Result, very rarely used like כִּי (cf. § 526), e.g.

אֲשֶׁר לֹא־יֹאמְרוּ זֹאת אִיזֶבֶל (II Kg 9/37); cf. Gn 13/16, I Kg 3/12 f.

466 (iv) Purpose, a very rare use (cf. § 522), e.g. אֲשֶׁר לֹא־ תִגָּלֶה עֶרְוָתְךָ עָלָיו (Ex 20/26); cf. Dt 4/40, Jo 3/7.

467 (v) Recitative, used like כִּי (cf. § 452) and Greek ὅτι to introduce direct speech (a rare use), e.g. וַיֹּאמֶר שָׁאוּל אֶל־שְׁמוּאֵל אֲשֶׁר שָׁמַעְתִּי בְּקוֹל יְ (I Sm 15/20); cf. II Sm 1/4.

468 (vi) Causal, introducing a noun clause probably equiva-lent to an accusative of specification, meaning 'in that . . .,' hence employed like כִּי (cf. § 532), e.g. וַיָּמָת בֶּן־הָאִשָּׁה הַזֹּאת לָיְלָה אֲשֶׁר שָׁכְבָה עָלָיו (I Kg 3/19); cf. I Sm 15/15, Gn 34/13, Jo 4/23.

469 (vii) Conditional, very rarely used like כִּי (cf. § 446) in real conditions, e.g. אֲשֶׁר תִּשְׁמְעוּ אֶל־מִצְוֹת יְ (Dt 11/27 ‖ כִּי in v. 28), אֲשֶׁר יִשְׁאָלוּן בְּנֵיכֶם מָחָר (Jo 4/21 ‖ אִם in v. 6). This is to be construed as a noun clause in an accusative function in the light of אֵת אֲשֶׁר יֶחֱטָא אִישׁ לְרֵעֵהוּ (I Kg 8/31 ‖ אִם in II Ch 6/22).

(b) The Particle שֶׁ/שַׁ·

470 In north Palestinian and late Hebrew the original rela-tive pronoun שַׁ·/שֶׁ was in use, but since it no longer exhibited distinctions of gender or number it may be re-garded as a particle (cf. § 129). Its uses parallel those of אֲשֶׁר (cf. § 462).

471 (i) Relative, e.g. כַּחוֹל שֶׁעַל־שְׂפַת הַיָּם (Ju 7/12), מַה־שֶּׁהָיָה הוּא שֶׁיִּהְיֶה (Ec 1/9).

78

472　(ii) Nominalizing, e.g. וְעָשִׂיתָ לִּי אֹת שָׁאַתָּה מְדַבֵּר עִמִּי (Ju
　　 6/17), וְרָאִיתִי אָנִי שֶׁיֵּשׁ יִתְרוֹן (Ec 2/13);　cf. Ec 2/14;
　　 so also after prepositions, e.g. בְּ (Ec 2/16), כְּ (Ec
　　 9/12, 10/3), עַד (Ju 5/7).

473　(iii) Result, e.g. מַה־דּוֹרֵךְ מְהֹדוֹר שֶׁכָּכָה הִשְׁבַּעְתָּנוּ (Ca 5/9),
　　 מֶה הָיָה שֶׁהַיָּמִים הָרִאשֹׁנִים הָיוּ טוֹבִים מֵאֵלֶּה (Ec 7/10).

474　(iv) Causal, with a noun clause equivalent to an accu-
　　 sative of specification (cf. § 468), e.g. שֶׁאֲנִי חָרֵגוּ
　　 (Ec 2/18), אַל־תִּרְאוּנִי שֶׁאֲנִי שְׁחַרְחֹרֶת שֶׁשֱּׁזָפַתְנִי הַשָּׁמֶשׁ (Ca
　　 1/6);　cf. Ca 5/2.

6. Accusative Particle אֵת

475　　The particle אֵת, rare in poetry but normal in prose,
　　 serves to introduce a determinated substantive, pronoun
　　 or clause when in the accusative function, e.g. בְּרֵאשִׁית
　　 בָּרָא אֱלֹהִים אֵת הַשָּׁמַיִם וְאֵת הָאָרֶץ (Gn 1/1), וַיְבָרֶךְ אֹתָם אֱלֹהִים
　　 (Gn 1/22);　cf. II Kg 8/5.　Occasionally it is incor-
　　 rectly used with an undeterminated accusative, e.g. וַיַּעַשׂ
　　 אֶת־בֵּית בָּמוֹת (I Kg 12/31);　cf. II Sm 4/11.　It is also
　　 employed with the accusative of specification (cf. § 57),
　　 e.g. חָלָה אֶת־רַגְלָיו (I Kg 15/23);　cf. I Sm 24/19;　the
　　 emphatic accusative of specification (cf. § 58), e.g.
　　 וַיַּרְא אֱלֹהִים אֶת־הָאוֹר כִּי־טוֹב (Gn 1/4);　the determinative
　　 accusative (cf. § 59), e.g. וַיֻּגַּד לְרִבְקָה אֶת־דִּבְרֵי עֵשָׂו (Gn
　　 27/42);　cf. I Kg 18/13;　the temporal accusative (cf.
　　 § 56), e.g. מַצּוֹת יֵאָכֵל אֵת שִׁבְעַת הַיָּמִים (Ex 13/7);　the
　　 accusative of material (cf. § 53), e.g. וַתִּמָּלֵא הָאָרֶץ אֵת־

הַמַּיִם (II Kg 3/20). The particle אֵת occurs with מִי, but never with מָה.

7. Existential Particle יֵשׁ

476 (a) Occasionally used in its original function of substantive, e.g. לְהַנְחִיל אֹהֲבַי יֵשׁ (Pr 8/21); cf. Si
25/21, 42/3.

477 (b) Expressing existence, e.g. יֵשׁ נָבִיא בְּיִשְׂרָאֵל (II Kg
5/8), אוּלַי יֵשׁ חֲמִשִּׁים צַדִּיקִם בְּתוֹךְ הָעִיר (Gn 18/24); so
with a noun clause, e.g. וְיֵשׁ אֲשֶׁר יִהְיֶה הֶעָנָן יָמִים מִסְפָּר
עַל־הַמִּשְׁכָּן (Nu 9/20); cf. Nu 9/21.

478 (c) Expressing possession, with the preposition לְ (cf.
§ 270), e.g. יֵשׁ־לָנוּ אָב זָקֵן (Gn 44/20), יֵשׁ אֱלֹהִים לְיִשְׂרָאֵל
(I Sm 17/46); cf. II Kg 4/2.

479 (d) Occasionally employed to introduce the pronominal
subject of a participle, e.g. לָדַעַת הֲיִשְׁכֶם אֹהֲבִים אֶת־יְ׳
(Dt 13/4); especially after אִם when the construction
expresses intention, e.g. אִם־יֶשְׁךָ־נָּא מַצְלִיחַ דַּרְכִּי (Gn
24/42); cf. Gn 43/4.

480 (e) Expressing obligation, with a construct infinitive,
e.g. הֲיֵשׁ לְדַבֶּר־לָךְ אֶל־הַמֶּלֶךְ (II Kg 4/13); cf. II Ch 25/9
(with the לְ of obligation; cf. § 284). This is a
variant of the gerundive use of the construct infinitive (cf. § 196).

481 (f) Elliptic, e.g. וַתֹּאמַרְנָה יֵשׁ (I Sm 9/12); cf. II Kg
10/15.

V. SYNTAX OF CLAUSES

482　Semitic languages, in contrast to Indo-European languages,
express logical subordination normally by grammatical co-
ordination, i.e. parataxis.

1.　Noun Clauses

483　Certain clauses are regarded by native Semitic grammarians as equivalent in function to nouns.　Such clauses
may, on rare occasions, be determinated by the article (cf.
§ 91), and when equivalent to an accusative case may also
be marked by the particle אֵת (cf. § 475).　They are frequently introduced by אֲשֶׁר (cf. § 464) or כִּי (cf. § 451).
It should be stressed that the case names merely express
syntactic functions.

(a) Nominative

484　(i) As subject of a verb, e.g. וּלְשָׁאוּל הֻגַּד כִּי־נִמְלַט דָּוִד
מִקְּעִילָה (I Sm 23/13);　cf. I Sm 27/4, and often after
וַיְהִי, e.g. וַיְהִי . . . נָתַן י' אֵלַי אֶת־שְׁנֵי לֻחֹת הָאֲבָנִים (Dt
9/11);　cf. Is 7/1;　more usually introduced by waw-
'consecutive' (e.g. Gn 21/22).

485　(ii) In apposition to a nominative substantive, e.g.
וְהִנֵּה אֱמֶת נָכוֹן הַדָּבָר נֶעֶשְׂתָה הַתּוֹעֵבָה הַזֹּאת בְּקִרְבֶּךָ (Dt 13/15,
17/4).

486　(iii) As a predicate nominative, e.g. וְזֶה אֲשֶׁר תַּעֲשֶׂה אֹתָהּ

81

(Gn 6/15);　cf. Ex 29/38.

487　(iv) As subject of an interrogative sentence, e.g. הֲכִי
יֶשׁ־עוֹד אֲשֶׁר נוֹתַר לְבֵית שָׁאוּל (II Sm 9/1);　cf. Gn 3/1.

488　(v) With an adjectival predicate, e.g. טוֹב אֲשֶׁר לֹא־תִדֹּר
(Ec 5/4);　cf. Ec 7/18.

  (b) Genitive

489　Clauses in this relationship are always asyndetic.
They may occur after a substantive in the bound form,
either with introductory אֲשֶׁר, e.g. מְקוֹם אֲשֶׁר־אֲסוּרֵי הַמֶּלֶךְ
אֲסוּרִים (Gn 39/20);　cf. Gn 40/3, Lv 13/46, Nu 9/18;　or
without, e.g. תְּחִלַּת דִּבֶּר־יְ' בְּהוֹשֵׁעַ (Ho 1/2);　cf. Gn 1/1,
Lv 7/35, I Sm 25/15, II Kg 8/6;　or they may follow a
preposition with no introductory particle, e.g. וְהָיָה
עֵקֶב תִּשְׁמְעוּן אֵת הַמִּשְׁפָּטִים הָאֵלֶּה (Dt 7/12);　cf. Nu 20/12,
Jb 16/17, Am 2/8, Gn 31/20, or introduced by אֲשֶׁר, e.g.
עַל כִּי־עָשׂוּ אַחֲרֵי אֲשֶׁר־הֵנִיחַ יְ' לְיִשְׂרָאֵל (Jo 23/1), or כִּי, e.g.
אֶת־הָרַע בְּעֵינֵי יְ' (Ju 3/12).

  (c) Accusative

490　(i) As object of a verb, usually with כִּי, e.g. וַיִּרָא יְ'
כִּי רַבָּה רָעַת הָאָדָם בָּאָרֶץ (Gn 6/5);　cf. Dt 16/12, or (אֵת)
אֲשֶׁר, e.g. וַיִּרָא שָׁאוּל אֲשֶׁר־הוּא מַשְׂכִּיל מְאֹד (I Sm 18/15);
cf. I Sm 24/11, II Kg 8/5, 12, but occasionally with-
out, e.g. מָה רְאִיתֶם עָשִׂיתִי מַהֲרוּ עֲשׂוּ כָמוֹנִי (Ju 9/48).
Clauses may also occur in apposition to an accusative
substantive, e.g. לֹא־יָדְעוּ . . . אֶת־גָּדְלוֹ . . . וַאֲשֶׁר
עָשָׂה לְחֵיל מִצְרַיִם (Dt 11/2-4).

491　(ii) In the adverbial accusative of manner (cf. § 60),

82

often to be rendered 'by . . .-ing.' Such clauses
are usually asyndetic with a finite verb and inverted
word order, e.g. וַיָּבֹא אֲלֵיהֶם יְהוֹשֻׁעַ פִּתְאֹם כָּל־הַלַּיְלָה עָלָה
מִן־הַגִּלְגָּל (Jo 10/9); cf. Dt 12/22, 7/6, Ex 16/18. In
some cases there is no inversion, e.g. וְהִנֵּה חֲטָאתֶם לַי׳
אֱלֹהֵיכֶם עֲשִׂיתֶם לָכֶם עֵגֶל מַסֵּכָה סַרְתֶּם מַהֵר מִן־הַדֶּרֶךְ אֲשֶׁר־צִוָּה י׳
אֶתְכֶם (Dt 9/16); cf. Dt 7/24. Occasionally the con-
junction is used, e.g. וַיַּעֲשׂוּ בְנֵי־יִשְׂרָאֵל אֶת־הָרַע בְּעֵינֵי
י׳ וַיַּעַבְדוּ אֶת־הַבְּעָלִים (Ju 2/11 f.); cf. Am 7/12. For
such clauses in the negative, either לֹא or אַל may be
employed, e.g. וַיַּעֲשֶׂה הָרַע בְּעֵינֵי י׳ לֹא סָר מִכָּל־חַטֹּאות
חָזַק . . . לַעֲשׂוֹת כְּכָל־הַתּוֹרָה (II Kg 13/11), . . . יָרָבְעָם
אַל־תָּסוּר מִמֶּנּוּ יָמִין וּשְׂמֹאול (Jo 1/7).

492 (iii) As an accusative of specification (cf. § 57), always with אֲשֶׁר (אֵת), e.g. אֲשֶׁר יֵאָמֵר הַיּוֹם, 'as it is said
today' (Gn 22/14), אֲשֶׁר בֵּרַכְךָ י׳ אֱלֹהֶיךָ, 'as Yahweh your
God has blessed you'(Dt 12/7), אֲשֶׁר־שָׂם לוֹ בַּדֶּרֶךְ, 'in
opposing them in the way' (I Sm 15/2); cf. Lv 26/35.
An instructive example is the following: עָשָׂה י׳ אֲשֶׁר
זָמָם בִּצַּע אֶמְרָתוֹ אֲשֶׁר צִוָּה מִימֵי־קֶדֶם הָרַס וְלֹא חָמָל, in which
אֲשֶׁר זָמָם is object of the verb, וְלֹא חָמָל is an adverbial
accusative, and אֲשֶׁר צִוָּה מִימֵי־קֶדֶם is an accusative of
specification, i.e. 'Yahweh has done what he planned,
has carried out his promise; as he decreed long ago,
he has demolished without pity' (La 2/17).

493 (iv) As a determinative accusative (cf. § 59), introduced by אֲשֶׁר, e.g. הֲלֹא־הֻגַּד לַאדֹנִי אֵת אֲשֶׁר־עָשִׂיתִי (I Kg
18/13); cf. II Sm 21/11.

83

2. Circumstantial Clauses

494   Clauses describing concomitant circumstances are introduced by the conjunction וְ of accompaniment (cf. § 436), which is occasionally omitted, then the subject followed by a participle (cf. § 219), except in the case of the verb 'to be,' or rarely a finite verbal form. Examples with a participle: וְהָהָר בֹּעֵר בָּאֵשׁ (Dt 5/23); cf. II Kg 8/7, Ex 22/9 (asyndetic); without a verbal form: וְרֹאשׁוֹ בַשָּׁמַיִם (Gn 11/4), פֶּסַח הוּא לַי'/ (Ex 12/11, asyndetic and with the copula הוּא); with a perfect aspect: וִי'/ הִצְלִיחַ דַּרְכִּי (Gn 24/56); cf. Gn 1/2, 26/27, II Kg 3/22; with an imperfect aspect: וְאַבְרָהָם הָיוֹ יִהְיֶה לְגוֹי גָּדוֹל וְעָצוּם (Gn 18/18).

3. Temporal Clauses

495   (a) Simple juxtaposition, meaning 'when,' e.g. וַתְּכַל לְהַשְׁקֹתוֹ וַתֹּאמֶר (Gn 24/19).

496   (b) Introduced by the conjunction כִּי, with the meaning 'when' (cf. § 445), e.g. וַיְהִי כִּי אָרְכוּ־לוֹ שָׁם הַיָּמִים (Gn 26/8).

497   (c) Introduced by prepositions followed by noun clauses with or without אֲשֶׁר:

498   (i) בְּ, 'when' (cf. § 241), e.g. בְּעוֹדֶנּוּ חַי (Gn 25/6); cf. Am 4/7. This is never used before a clause introduced by אֲשֶׁר.

499   (ii) (מוֹ)כְּ, 'as soon as,' or (אֲשֶׁר)כְּ, simply 'when'

84

(cf. § 262;   the meaning has weakened since there is

no contrast with *(בַּאֲשֶׁר), e.g. וּכְמוֹ הַשַּׁחַר עָלָה (Gn

19/15), כַּאֲשֶׁר כִּלּוּ הַגְּמַלִּים לִשְׁתּוֹת (Gn 24/22).

500   (iii) אַחֲרֵי, 'after' (cf. § 360), e.g. אַחֲרֵי הֵסַבּוּ אֹתוֹ

(I Sm 5/9);   cf. Jo 9/16.

501   (iv) עַד, 'until' (cf. § 311), e.g. עַד אֲשֶׁר לֹא־נוֹתְרָה־בּוֹ

נְשָׁמָה (I Kg 17/17).

502 (d) Expressed by prepositions with an infinitive:

503   (i) בְּ, 'when' (cf. § 241), e.g. בְּעׇמְדוֹ לִפְנֵי פַרְעֹה (Gn

41/46).

504   (ii) כְּ, 'as soon as' (cf. § 262), e.g. כְּבוֹא אַבְרָם

מִצְרָיְמָה (Gn 12/14).

505   (iii) אַחֲרֵי, 'after' (cf. § 360), e.g. אַחֲרֵי שׁוּבוֹ מֵהַכּוֹת

אֶת־כְּדָר־לָעֹמֶר (Gn 14/17).

506   (iv) לִפְנֵי, 'before' (cf. § 371), e.g. לִפְנֵי בוֹא־הַשֶּׁמֶשׁ

(II Sm 3/35).

507   (v) עַד, 'until' (cf. § 311), e.g. עַד־שׁוּב אַף־אָחִיךָ מִמְּךָ

(Gn 27/45).

508 (e) By means of the expression (בְּ)טֶרֶם, 'before,' and a

noun clause with the imperfect aspect (cf. § 167),

either indicating past time, e.g. בְּטֶרֶם תָּבוֹא וָאֲבָרֲכֵהוּ

(Gn 27/33);   cf. Gn 19/4;   or future time, e.g. וְאֶרְאֶנּוּ

בְּטֶרֶם אָמוּת (Gn 45/28).

509 (f) By the expression מִדֵּי, 'as often as,' with an in-

finitive, e.g. וַיְהִי מִדֵּי־בֹא הַמֶּלֶךְ בֵּית י׳ (I Kg 14/28),

or with a noun clause and the imperfect aspect, e.g.

85

כִּי־מִדֵּי אֲדַבֵּר אֶזְעָק (Je 20/8).

4. Conditional Clauses

510 The apodosis is usually introduced by the resumptive
ן (cf. § 440); note, however, II Kg 4/29, Gn 18/3, etc.).
Occasionally אָז is used in real or unreal conditions (e.g.
Pr 2/5, II Sm 19/7).

(a) Real Conditions

511 (i) By simple juxtaposition (virtual conditional), e.g.
וְעָזַב אֶת־אָבִיו וָמֵת (Gn 44/22); cf. I Sm 19/3.

512 (ii) By means of a circumstantial clause (cf. § 494),
e.g. הִנֵּה יְ׳ עֹשֶׂה אֲרֻבּוֹת בַּשָּׁמַיִם הֲיִהְיֶה הַדָּבָר הַזֶּה (II Kg 7/2);
cf. Ex 3/13.

513 (iii) With the particle הֵן (cf. Aramaic and הִנֵּה in
§ 512), e.g. הֵן צַדִּיק בָּאָרֶץ יְשֻׁלָּם (Pr 11/31).

514 (iv) With the particles אִם (cf. § 453) or כִּי (cf. § 446),
expressing past time (with the perfect aspect), e.g.
כִּי שָׁטִית תַּחַת אִישֵׁךְ וְכִי (Gn 18/3), אִם־נָא מָצָאתִי חֵן בְּעֵינֶיךָ
נִטְמָאה (Nu 5/20); past frequentative time (with the
imperfect aspect), e.g. וְאִם־לֹא יֵעָלֶה הֶעָנָן (Ex 40/37);
future time (with the imperfect aspect), e.g. אִם־יִהְיֶה
אֱלֹהִים עִמָּדִי (Gn 28/20); imminent future or present
time (with the participle), e.g. אִם־לֹקֵחַ יַעֲקֹב אִשָּׁה (Gn
27/46), כִּי־אֵינְךָ יוֹצֵא (II Sm 19/8); present frequentative time (with the imperfect aspect), e.g. וְאִם לֹא
תֵיטִיב (Gn 4/7). Very rarely the particle אֲשֶׁר is employed (cf. § 469), e.g. אֲשֶׁר תִּשְׁמְעוּ אֶל־מִצְוֹת יְ׳ (Dt

86

11/27);   cf. Jo 4/21.

(b) Unreal Conditions

515   (i) With the particle לוּ (cf. § 459), usually in past

time (with the perfect aspect), e.g. לוּ הַחֲיִתֶם אוֹתָם

(Ju 8/19);   cf. Ju 13/23;   the negative is expressed

by לוּלֵי/לוּלֵא, e.g. לוּלֵא הִתְמַהְמָהְנוּ (Gn 43/10).   Rarely

in present or future time (with a participle), e.g.

וְלֹא אָנֹכִי שֹׁקֵל עַל־כַּפַּי אֶלֶף כָּסֶף (II Sm 18/12);   cf. II Sm

19/7;   in the negative, לוּלֵי פְּנֵי יְהוֹשָׁפָט . . . אֲנִי

נֹשֵׂא (II Kg 3/14).   In late times אִלּוּ is used, e.g.

וְאִלּוּ חָיָה אֶלֶף שָׁנִים פַּעֲמַיִם (Ec 6/6);   cf. Es 7/4.

516   (ii) Exceptionally with the particles כִּי (e.g. Ru

1/12) or אָם (e.g. Ps 50/12);   cf. §§ 446, 453.

5. Telic (Final or Purpose) Clauses

517   (a) By means of 'simple' waw and the precative mood (cf.

§ 187), e.g. וְהָבִיאָה לִּי וְאֹכֵלָה (Gn 27/4);   cf. Lv 9/6.

518   (b) By means of waw and the imperative mood (cf. § 189),

e.g. מָה אֶעֱשֶׂה לָכֶם . . . וּבָרְכוּ אֶת־נַחֲלַת יְ' (II Sm 21/3);

cf. Is 45/22.

519   (c) By לְ and the construct infinitive (cf. § 197), e.g.

וַיַּעֲלֶה אַחְאָב לֶאֱכֹל וְלִשְׁתּוֹת (I Kg 18/42), or לְמַעַן with the

infinitive (cf. § 367), e.g. וְיָד אַל־תִּשְׁלְחוּ־בוֹ לְמַעַן הַצִּיל

אֹתוֹ מִיָּדָם (Gn 37/22).

520   (d) By לְמַעַן with a noun clause (with or without אֲשֶׁר)

and the imperfect aspect (cf. §§ 175, 367), e.g.

נִשְׁמַע לְמַעַן אֲשֶׁר יִיטַב־לָנוּ (Je 42/6);   cf. Gn 12/13.

521   (e) By בַּעֲבוּר with the infinitive, e.g. בַּעֲבוּר זֹאת הֶעֱמַדְתִּיךָ
בַּעֲבוּר הַרְאֹתְךָ אֶת־כֹּחִי (Ex 9/16); cf. II Sm 10/3 (also
pleonastically לְבַעֲבוּר, e.g. II Sm 14/20, Ex 20/20),
or with a noun clause (with or without אֲשֶׁר), e.g.
וְהֵבֵאתָ לְאָבִיךָ וְאָכָל בַּעֲבֻר אֲשֶׁר יְבָרֶכְךָ לִפְנֵי מוֹתוֹ (Gn 27/10);
cf. Gn 27/4, 21/30.

522   (f) Very rarely by means of the particle אֲשֶׁר and a noun
clause (cf. § 466), e.g. וְשָׁמַרְתָּ אֶת־חֻקָּיו . . . אֲשֶׁר יִיטַב
לְךָ וּלְבָנֶיךָ אַחֲרֶיךָ (Dt 4/40); cf. Jo 3/7.

523   (g) Negative purpose is expressed by לְבִלְתִּי with a noun
clause containing an imperfect aspect (cf. § 424),
e.g. כִּי לְבַעֲבוּר נַסּוֹת אֶתְכֶם בָּא הָאֱלֹהִים . . . לְבִלְתִּי תֶחֱטָאוּ
(Ex 20/20); cf. II Sm 14/14; or with a construct
infinitive (cf. § 423), e.g. וַיָּשֶׂם יְ׳ לְקַיִן אוֹת לְבִלְתִּי
הַכּוֹת־אֹתוֹ כָּל־מֹצְאוֹ (Gn 4/15); cf. II Kg 23/10. Rarely,
לְמַעַן (אֲשֶׁר) לֹא with a noun clause (cf. § 367) is used,
e.g. לְמַעַן אֲשֶׁר לֹא־יִקְרַב אִישׁ זָר (Nu 17/5); cf. Ezk 14/11.

6.   Result Clauses

524   (a) By means of a simple consecutive sequence (cf.
§§ 178 f.), e.g. וַיִּסְקְלֻהוּ בָאֲבָנִים וַיָּמֹת (I Kg 21/13).

525   (b) By a construct infinitive with לְ, e.g. וּלְחַלֵּל אֶת־שֵׁם
קָדְשִׁי (Lv 20/3), or rarely לְמַעַן (cf. § 198).

526   (c) With a noun clause introduced by כִּי (cf. § 450),
e.g. וְאַהֲרֹן מַה־הוּא כִּי תַלּוֹנוּ עָלָיו (Nu 16/11); cf. Gn
20/10, or rarely by אֲשֶׁר (cf. § 465), e.g. אֲשֶׁר לֹא־הָיָה
כָמוֹךָ אִישׁ בַּמְּלָכִים כָּל־יָמֶיךָ (I Kg 3/13).

7. Concessive Clauses

527　(a) By means of a circumstantial clause (cf. § 494),

e.g. הִנֵּה־נָא הוֹאַלְתִּי לְדַבֵּר אֶל־אֲדֹנָי וְאָנֹכִי עָפָר וָאֵפֶר (Gn

18/27);　cf. Ju 16/15.

528　(b) By means of the conjunction אִם (cf. § 454), e.g.

אִם־צָדַקְתִּי לֹא אֶעֱנֶה (Jb 9/15);　cf. Am 9/2-4.

529　(c) By means of גַּם כִּי, e.g. גַּם כִּי־תַרְבּוּ תְפִלָּה אֵינֶנִּי שֹׁמֵעַ

(Is 1/15), or simply כִּי (cf. § 448), e.g. כִּי־יִפֹּל לֹא־

יוּטָל (Ps 37/24), or גַּם (cf. § 382), e.g. רַבַּת צְרָרוּנִי

מִנְּעוּרָי גַּם לֹא־יָכְלוּ לִי (Ps 129/2).

530　(d) By means of the preposition עַל with a noun clause

(cf. § 288), e.g. עַל לֹא־חָמָס עָשָׂה (Is 53/9);　cf. Jb

16/17, or with an infinitive, e.g. עַל־דַּעְתְּךָ כִּי־לֹא אֶרְשָׁע

(Jb 10/7).

531　(e) By the preposition כְּ (cf. § 258) with an infinitive,

e.g. וַיְהִי כְּדַבְּרָהּ אֶל־יוֹסֵף יוֹם יוֹם (Gn 39/10).

8. Causal Clauses

532　(a) By means of the conjunction כִּי (cf. § 444), e.g. קֵץ

כָּל־בָּשָׂר בָּא לְפָנַי כִּי־מָלְאָה הָאָרֶץ חָמָס מִפְּנֵיהֶם (Gn 6/13), or

the particle אֲשֶׁר (cf. § 468), e.g. מֵעֲמָלֵקִי הֱבִיאוּם אֲשֶׁר

חָמַל הָעָם עַל־מֵיטַב הַצֹּאן וְהַבָּקָר (I Sm 15/15);　cf. II Sm

2/5.

533　(b) By means of a preposition followed by a noun clause,

viz. (אֲשֶׁר/כִּי) יַעַן (cf. § 363), e.g. יַעַן כִּי גָבְהוּ בְּנוֹת

צִיּוֹן (Is 3/16);　cf. Nu 20/12, Gn 22/16;　(אֲשֶׁר/כִּי)־עַל

(cf. § 291), e.g. עַל לֹא־שָׁמְרוּ תוֹרָתֶךָ (Ps 119/136);　cf.

89

עֵקֶב הָיְתָה, e.g. עֵקֶב (אֲשֶׁר/כִּי) II Sm 3/30, Ju 3/12;

רוּחַ אַחֶרֶת עִמֹּו (Nu 14/24); cf. Gn 22/18, II Sm 12/10;

בַּ(אֲשֶׁר) (cf. § 247), e.g. בַּאֲשֶׁר יְ אִתֹּו (Gn 39/23); cf.

Gn 39/9; כַּ(אֲשֶׁר) (cf. § 260), e.g. וְהָעָם מְמִיתִים אֹותָם

כַּאֲשֶׁר אֵינָם יֹדְעִים אֶת־מִשְׁפַּט אֱלֹהֵי הָאָרֶץ (II Kg 17/26); cf.

I Sm 28/18, Nu 27/14; מִ(אֲשֶׁר) (cf. § 319), e.g. מֵאֲשֶׁר

יָקַרְתָּ בְעֵינַי (Is 43/4); תַּחַת (אֲשֶׁר/כִּי) (cf. § 353), e.g.

תַּחַת כִּי־שָׂנְאוּ דָעַת (Pr 1/29); cf. Nu 25/13, II Kg 22/17;

מִפְּנֵי (אֲשֶׁר) (cf. § 376), e.g. מִפְּנֵי אֲשֶׁר קִטְּרָתֶם (Je 44/23);

cf. Ex 19/18.

534 (c) By means of a preposition with a construct infini-

tive, viz. יַעַן (cf. § 363), e.g. יַעַן הִתְרַגֶּזְךָ אֵלַי

(II Kg 19/28); cf. I Kg 21/20; עַל (cf. § 291), e.g.

עַל־מִכְרָם בַּכֶּסֶף צַדִּיק (Am 2/6); cf. Am 1/9; בְּ (cf. § 247),

e.g. הֲלֹוא בְלֶכְתְּךָ עִמָּנוּ (Ex 33/16); cf. I Kg 18/18; מִן

(cf. § 319), e.g. מִיִּרְאָתֹו אֹתֹו (II Sm 3/11); cf. Dt

7/7.

9. Relative Clauses

535 (a) Occasionally in poetry expressed by the obsolescent

relative pronouns זוּ, זֹו, זֶה (cf. § 129), e.g. בְּרֶשֶׁת־

זוּ טָמָנוּ (Ps 9/16); cf. Jb 19/19.

536 (b) By means of the dialectal relative pronoun שֶׁ (cf.

§§ 129, 470 f.) in north Palestinian and late Hebrew,

e.g. מִי מִשֶּׁלָּנוּ (II Kg 6/11); cf. Ju 7/12, Ec 1/9.

537 (c) Usually by means of the relative particle אֲשֶׁר (cf.

§§ 462 f.), rare in poetry, e.g. הַמָּקֹום אֲשֶׁר אַתָּה עֹומֵד

עָלָיו (Ex 3/5).

538   (d) By means of the article before a participle or a

clause with a finite verb (cf. §§ 90 f.), e.g. וְאֶל־

מֶלֶךְ יְהוּדָה הַשֹּׁלֵחַ אֶתְכֶם לִדְרֹשׁ אֶת־יְ׳ (II Kg 22/18);   cf.

Is 8/6;   הַנִּרְאָה אֵלָיו פַּעֲמָיִם (I Kg 11/9);   cf. Ez 10/17.

539   (e) By means of parataxis or simple juxtaposition of

clauses (virtual relative), a construction common in

poetry (originally employed when the antecedent was

undeterminated, as in Arabic), e.g. יֹאבַד יוֹם אִוָּלֶד בּוֹ

וְהַלַּיְלָה אָמַר הֹרָה גָבֶר (Jb 3/3);   cf. Dt 32/17, Is 40/20,

Je 13/20, Ps 18/44. This is occasionally found also

in prose, e.g. אֶת־הַדֶּרֶךְ יֵלְכוּ בָהּ (Ex 18/20);   cf. Gn

15/13.

10.   Interrogative Clauses

540   (a) Direct questions are introduced by the particle הֲ,

e.g. הֲתֵלְכִי עִם־הָאִישׁ הַזֶּה (Gn 24/58);   cf. Gn 50/19.

541   (b) Sometimes they are expressed merely by intonation,

e.g. וַיֹּאמֶר שָׁלֹם בּוֹאֶךָ (I Sm 16/4);   cf. I Sm 11/12,

II Sm 11/11.

542   (c) Indirect questions are indicated by הֲ, e.g. לָדַעַת

הֲיִשְׁכֶם אֹהֲבִים אֶת־יְ׳ אֱלֹהֵיכֶם (Dt 13/4), or אִם, e.g. לְכוּ

דִּרְשׁוּ . . . אִם־אֶחְיֶה מֵחֳלִי זֶה (II Kg 1/2).

543   (d) Disjunctive questions are expressed by (וְ) . . .הֲ,

אִם, e.g. הַכֶּר־נָא הַכְּתֹנֶת בִּנְךָ הִוא אִם־לֹא (Gn 37/32);   cf.

Jb 22/3;   less frequently by הֲ . . . הֲ, e.g. הֶחָזָק הוּא

הֲרָפֶה (Nu 13/18);   or more rarely by אוֹ . . . הֲ, e.g.

91

וּמִי יוֹדֵעַ הֶחָכָם יִהְיֶה אוֹ סָכָל (Ec 2/19); cf. Ju 18/19.

544 (e) Interrogative pronouns or adverbs may be employed,

such as מִי, 'who?' מָה, 'what?' אָן, 'where?' אֵיךְ, 'how?'

11. Desiderative (Optative) Clauses

545 (a) Expressed by the precative mood (cf. § 184), e.g.

אָשִׂימָה עָלַי מֶלֶךְ כְּכָל־הַגּוֹיִם (Dt 17/14); cf. I Sm 1/23.

546 (b) By means of מִי־יִתֵּן with a construct infinitive, e.g.

מִי־יִתֵּן מוּתִי אֲנִי תַחְתֶּיךָ (II Sm 19/1); cf. Ex 16/3; a

perfect aspect, e.g. מִי־יִתֵּן יָדַעְתִּי וְאֶמְצָאֵהוּ (Jb 23/3);

an imperfect aspect, e.g. מִי יִתֵּן בִּשְׁאוֹל תַּצְפִּנֵנִי (Jb

14/13); cf. Jb 6/8; in such a case the main verb

may be introduced by waw-'consecutive,' e.g. מִי־יִתֵּן

וְהָיָה לְבָבָם זֶה לָהֶם (Dt 5/29); or in a non-verbal clause,

e.g. וּמִי יִתֵּן כָּל־עַם י' נְבִיאִים (Nu 11/29); cf. Dt 28/67.

Sometimes merely מִי is used (cf. § 122), e.g. מִי יַשְׁקֵנִי

מַיִם (II Sm 23/15); cf. II Sm 15/4.

547 (c) By means of לוּ (cf. § 460) with the imperfect aspect,

e.g. לוּ שָׁקוֹל יִשָּׁקֵל כַּעְשִׂי (Jb 6/2); cf. Gn 17/18; with

the perfect aspect, e.g. וְלוּ הוֹאַלְנוּ וַנֵּשֶׁב בְּעֵבֶר הַיַּרְדֵּן

(Jo 7/7); cf. Nu 14/2; with the precative mood, e.g.

לוּ יְהִי כִדְבָרֶךָ (Gn 30/34); in an existential sentence,

e.g. לוּ יֶשׁ־חֶרֶב בְּיָדִי (Nu 22/29).

548 (d) By means of אַחֲלֵי/אַחֲלַי, e.g. אֲחַלֵּי אֲדֹנִי לִפְנֵי הַנָּבִיא אֲשֶׁר

בְּשֹׁמְרוֹן (II Kg 5/3); cf. Ps 119/5.

549 (e) Rarely by means of אָם (cf. § 458), e.g. אִם־תִּקְטֹל אֱלוֹהַּ

רָשָׁע (Ps 139/19).

12. Adversative Clauses

550 (a) By means of the conjunction וְ (cf. § 432), e.g.

וְלֹא־יִקָּרֵא עוֹד אֶת־שִׁמְךָ אַבְרָם וְהָיָה שִׁמְךָ אַבְרָהָם (Gn 17/5);

cf. I Kg 3/11.

551 (b) By means of the adverb אוּלָם(וְ), e.g. וְאוּלָם אָחִיו

הַקָּטֹן יִגְדַּל מִמֶּנּוּ (Gn 48/19); cf. Ex 9/16, Jb 1/11, 2/5.

552 (c) The particle אֲבָל (only asseverative in classical

Hebrew) is used in late texts, e.g. אֲבָל אֲרוֹן הָאֱלֹהִים

הֶעֱלָה דָוִיד מִקִּרְיַת יְעָרִים (II Ch 1/4).

553 (d) By means of the conjunction כִּי after negatives (cf.

§ 447), e.g. כִּי־בוֹקֵר אָנֹכִי (Am 7/14); cf. Gn 17/15.

It is commonly reinforced with pleonastic אִם (cf.

§ 457), e.g. וַיֹּאמְרוּ לֹא כִּי אִם־מֶלֶךְ יִהְיֶה עָלֵינוּ (I Sm

8/19); cf. Ps 1/2, Dt 7/5.

13. Exceptive (Limitative) Clauses

554 (a) By means of כִּי אִם, after a negative or a rhetorical

question (cf. § 447), e.g. לֹא אֲשַׁלֵּחֲךָ כִּי אִם־בֵּרַכְתָּנִי (Gn

32/27); cf. Am 3/7, Lv 22/6.

555 (b) By means of בִּלְתִּי אִם (cf. § 422), e.g. הֲיִתֵּן כְּפִיר

קוֹלוֹ מִמְּעֹנָתוֹ בִּלְתִּי אִם־לָכָד (Am 3/4); also without ple-

onastic אִם, e.g. אֵין כֹּל בִּלְתִּי אֶל־הַמָּן עֵינֵינוּ (Nu 11/6);

cf. Gn 43/3, Is 10/4.

14. Restrictive Clauses

557 (a) By means of אֶפֶס כִּי (cf. § 427), e.g. אֶפֶס כִּי־עַז הָעָם

93

הַיֹּשֵׁב בָּאָרֶץ (Nu 13/28);   cf. Ju 4/9, Am 9/8.   When a
second פִּי would follow, the first is omitted, e.g.
אֶפֶס כִּי־נִאֵץ נִאַצְתָּ אֶת־אֹיְבֵי י' בַּדָּבָר הַזֶּה (II Sm 12/14).

558   (b) By means of the particle אַךְ (cf. § 388), e.g. אַךְ
הֱיֵה־לִּי לְבֶן־חַיִל (I Sm 18/17);   cf. I Kg 17/13, Gn 9/4.

559   (c) By means of the particle רַק (cf. § 390), e.g. רַק
לָאֲנָשִׁים הָאֵל אַל־תַּעֲשׂוּ דָבָר (Gn 19/8);   cf. Dt 12/15, I Kg
3/3.

15. Equational Clauses

560   These are non-verbal statements in present time, since
in past or future time the verb הָיָה is usually employed.

561   (a) With a substantival predicate, e.g. עֵד הַגַּל הַזֶּה (Gn
31/52), אֲנָשִׁים אַחִים אֲנָחְנוּ (Gn 13/8), אֵלֶּה שְׁמוֹת בְּנֵי־עֵשָׂו
(Gn 36/10), וַיְהִי־הֶבֶל רֹעֵה צֹאן (Gn 4/2).   This frequently occurs when an adjectival predicate might have
been expected, e.g. אֱמֶת הָיָה אֱמֶת נָכוֹן הַדָּבָר (Dt 13/15),
הֲשָׁלוֹם בָּאָה (I Kg 2/13), הַדָּבָר אֲשֶׁר שָׁמָעְתִּי (I Kg 10/6).
The negative is expressed by means of לֹא (contrast
non-existence with אַיִן, § 568), e.g. לֹא־אָחִיךָ הוּא (Dt
17/15), לֹא נָבִיא אָנֹכִי (Am 7/14), לֹא־חֹדֶשׁ וְלֹא שַׁבָּת (II Kg
4/23).

562   (b) With an adjectival predicate (cf. § 75), e.g. וְעֵינַי
רַבָּה רָעַת (I Sm 12/17), רְעַתְכֶם רַבָּה (Gn 29/17), לֵאָה רַכּוֹת
(Gn 6/5), וַיְהִי עֵר בְּכוֹר יְהוּדָה רַע בְּעֵינֵי י' הָאָדָם בָּאָרֶץ (Gn
38/7);   the negative is expressed with לֹא, e.g. לֹא־טוֹב
הַדָּבָר (Ex 18/17).

94

563   (c) With the preposition בְּ of identity (cf. § 249) be-

      fore a substantival predicate, e.g. כִּי־אֱלֹהֵי אָבִי בְּעֶזְרִי

      (Ex 18/4);   cf. Ps 29/4.

564   (d) With a prepositional phrase as predicate, e.g. הֵנֵּה־

      וּדְבַר־אַבְנֵר הָיָה עִם־זִקְנֵי יִשְׂרָאֵל (Gn 24/51), רִבְקָה לְפָנֶיךָ

      (II Sm 3/17);   with לֹא in the negative, e.g. לֹא בָרַעַשׁ

      יְ (I Kg 19/11);   cf. Nu 23/23.

565   (e) With an adverbial predicate, e.g. זֶבַח הַיָּמִים שָׁם

      (I Sm 20/6).

16.   Existential Clauses

566   (a) To express past or future time the verb הָיָה is em-

      ployed, e.g. אִישׁ הָיָה בְאֶרֶץ־עוּץ (Jb 1/1);   with לֹא in

      the negative, e.g. וְלֹא־הָיָה שָׁם לֶחֶם כִּי־אִם־לֶחֶם הַפָּנִים

      (I Sm 21/7).

567   (b) The particle יֵשׁ (cf. § 477) may be employed, e.g.

      וְגַם יֵשׁ גֹּאֵל קָרוֹב מִמֶּנִּי (Ru 3/12).

568   (c) Non-existence may be expressed by means of the nega-

      tive substantive אֵין (cf. §§ 407 f.), either in the

      bound form, e.g. בַּיָּמִים הָהֵם אֵין מֶלֶךְ בְּיִשְׂרָאֵל (Ju 21/25),

      or with the free form in apposition, e.g. וְכֹחַ אַיִן לְלֵדָה

      (II Kg 19/3).   In two passages the particle יֵשׁ is

      used redundantly with אֵין: וְאִין יֵשׁ־פֹּה תַּחַת־יָדְךָ חֲנִית

      אֹו־חֶרֶב (I Sm 21/9), אַף אֵין־יֵשׁ־רוּחַ בְּפִיהֶם (Ps 135/17).

      More rarely the substantive אֶפֶס (cf. § 426) may be em-

      ployed, either in the bound form, e.g. וְאֶפֶס עָצוּר וְאֶפֶס

      עָזוּב (II Kg 14/26), or with the free form in apposition, e.g. הַאֶפֶס עוֹד אִישׁ לְבֵית שָׁאוּל (II Sm 9/3).

17. Word Order

569   With the loss of case endings, word order became an
important feature of Hebrew syntax (see pp. 3 f.).

570   (a) <u>Verbal Clauses</u>, which are those containing verbal
forms other than participles or infinitives.

571   (i) The normal order is verbal predicate + noun subject + noun object + adverb or prepositional phrase,
e.g. וַיָּבֵא יוֹסֵף אֶת־דִּבָּתָם רָעָה אֶל־אֲבִיהֶם (Gn 37/2), וַיִּבְרָא
אֱלֹהִים אֶת־הָאָדָם בְּצַלְמוֹ (Gn 1/27); cf. Gn 2/8. Expressions of time are usually placed at the beginning,
e.g. בְּעֵת הַהִיא אָמַר י׳ אֶל־יְהוֹשֻׁעַ (Jo 5/2), בַּיָּמִים הָהֵם
חָלָה חִזְקִיָּהוּ לָמוּת (II Kg 20/1). Pronominal objects
or prepositions with suffixes may intervene between
verb and subject, e.g. וְלֹא־נָשָׂא אֹתָם הָאָרֶץ לָשֶׁבֶת יַחְדָּו
(Gn 13/6), וַיֹּאמֶר לָהֶם יוֹסֵף (Gn 44/15). Sometimes the
position of subject and object is reversed, e.g.
וַיַּחְנְכוּ אֶת־בֵּית י׳ הַמֶּלֶךְ וְכָל־בְּנֵי יִשְׂרָאֵל (I Kg 8/63).

572   (ii) The subject may precede the verb: (1) for emphasis, e.g. אֱלֹהִים יִרְאֶה־לּוֹ הַשֶּׂה (Gn 3/13), הַנָּחָשׁ הִשִּׁיאַנִי
לְעֹלָה (Gn 22/8); (2) for contrast, e.g. אַבְרָם יָשַׁב
בְּאֶרֶץ־כְּנַעַן וְלוֹט יָשַׁב בְּעָרֵי הַכִּכָּר (Gn 13/12), וְחַנָּה לֹא
עָלָתָה (I Sm 1/22); cf. Gn 37/11, 4/2; (3) to indi-
cate a change of subject, e.g. וּמַלְכִּי־צֶדֶק מֶלֶךְ שָׁלֵם
הוֹצִיא לֶחֶם וָיַיִן (Gn 14/18), וְרִבְקָה אָמְרָה אֶל־יַעֲקֹב בְּנָהּ
(Gn 27/6); (4) to express anterior time (equivalent

96

to an English pluperfect (cf. § 162, 3), e.g. וְנֹ֫חַ מָצָא
חֵן בְּעֵינֵי יְ׳ (Gn 6/8); cf. Gn 31/25; (5) to indicate
synchronism (cf. §§ 235, 237), e.g. ה֖וּא־בָ֥א עַד־לֶ֔חִי
וּפְלִשְׁתִּ֖ים הֵרִ֥יעוּ לִקְרָאתוֹ (Ju 15/14); (6) when lengthy, it
may be placed in rhetorical exposure (cf. § 35), e.g.
הָֽאִשָּׁ֗ה אֲשֶׁ֤ר נָתַ֫תָּה עִמָּדִ֔י הִ֛וא נָֽתְנָה־לִּ֥י מִן־הָעֵ֖ץ (Gn 3/12); cf.
Ju 13/8; (7) when the subject is an interrogative pro-
noun, e.g. מִ֣י יַֽעֲלֶה־לָּ֧נוּ אֶל־הַֽכְּנַעֲנִ֛י (Ju 1/1).

573 (iii) The object may precede the verb: (1) for emphasis,
e.g. אֶת־קֹלְךָ֥ שָׁמַ֖עְתִּי (II Kg 22/8), סֵ֧פֶר הַתּוֹרָ֛ה מָצָ֖אתִי בְּבֵ֥ית יְ׳
בַּגָּֽן (Gn 3/10); cf. I Sm 8/7; (2) when it is an in-
terrogative pronoun, e.g. מָֽה־אֶעֱשֶׂ֣ה לָאֵ֔לֶּה (Gn 31/43),
וְאֶת־מִ֤י עָשַׁ֙קְתִּי֙ אֶת־מִ֣י רַצּ֔וֹתִי (I Sm 12/3); (3) when stressed or cumbersome it may be placed in rhetorical ex-
posure, e.g. וְגַ֣ם אֶת־מַֽעֲכָ֣ה אִמּ֗וֹ וַיְסִרֶ֙הָ֙ מִגְּבִירָ֔ה (I Kg 15/13),
אֶת־אֲשֶׁ֨ר יֹאמַ֥ר יְ׳ אֵלַ֛י אֹת֖וֹ אֲדַבֵּֽר (I Kg 22/14); cf. II Kg
23/19, Gn 13/15.

574 (iv) A prepositional phrase may also precede the verb:
(1) for emphasis, e.g. בְּזֵעַ֤ת אַפֶּ֙יךָ֙ תֹּ֣אכַל לֶ֔חֶם (Gn 3/19),
בַּיַּבָּשָׁ֕ה עָבַ֥ר יִשְׂרָאֵ֖ל אֶת־הַיַּרְדֵּ֥ן הַזֶּֽה (Jo 4/22); cf. Gn 2/17;
(2) for contrast, e.g. וְאֶל־קַ֥יִן וְאֶל־מִנְחָת֖וֹ לֹ֣א שָׁעָ֑ה (Gn
4/5); cf. Gn 1/5; (3) when lengthy, it may be placed
in rhetorical exposure, e.g. הַמִּטָּ֞ה אֲשֶׁר־עָלִ֥יתָ שָּׁ֛ם לֹֽא־תֵרֵ֥ד
מִמֶּ֖נָּה (II Kg 1/4).

575 (v) In adverbial clauses (cf. § 491) the order subject +
object or prepositional phrase + verb may occur, e.g.
אִ֥ישׁ לְפִֽי־אָכְל֖וֹ לָקָ֑טוּ (Ju 17/6), אִ֥ישׁ הַיָּשָׁ֥ר בְּעֵינָ֖יו יַֽעֲשֶׂה (Ex
16/18).

97

(b) <u>Non-Verbal Clauses</u>

576   (i) The normal order is subject + predicate + adverb or
prepositional phrase, e.g. יֵצֶר לֵב הָאָדָם רַע מִנְּעֻרָיו (Gn
8/21), הֵמָּה הַגִּבֹּרִים (Gn 6/4), זֶה הַדָּבָר אֲשֶׁר עָשׂוּן (II Kg
11/5).

577   (ii) The predicate may precede for emphasis, e.g. עֵד הַגַּל
הַזֶּה (Gn 31/52), דָּם זֶה (II Kg 3/23); thus frequently
when the subject is a personal pronoun, e.g. אֲנָשִׁים
אַחִים אֲנַחְנוּ (Gn 13/8); cf. Gn 3/19, I Sm 15/29; when
the predicate is an adjective, e.g. טוֹב הָעֵץ לְמַאֲכָל (Gn
3/6), especially in a comparative statement, e.g. גָּדוֹל
עֲוֹנִי מִנְּשֹׂא (Gn 4/13); in a question, e.g. הֲלֹא טוֹב לָנוּ
שׁוּב מִצְרָיְמָה (Nu 14/3), אֵי הֶבֶל אָחִיךָ (Gn 4/9), and always
with an interrogative pronoun, e.g. מַה־שְּׁמוֹ (Ex 3/13),
מִי־הָאִישׁ הַלָּזֶה (Gn 24/65).

578   (iii) A prepositional phrase may precede for emphasis,
e.g. לַפֶּתַח חַטָּאת רֹבֵץ (Gn 4/7); so always if it con-
tains an interrogative pronoun, e.g. וּלְמִי כָּל־חֶמְדַּת
יִשְׂרָאֵל (I Sm 9/20).

18. Ellipsis

(a) In comparisons:

579   (i) Omission of a substantive, e.g. מְשַׁוֶּה רַגְלַי כָּאַיָּלוֹת,
'making my feet like (those of) hinds' (Ps 18/34 =
II Sm 22/34); cf. Ps 92/11.

580   (ii) Omission of a predicative adjective, e.g. וּפְסִילֵיהֶם
מִירוּשָׁלַם וּמִשֹּׁמְרוֹן, 'whose images were (greater than those

98

of) Jerusalem and Samaria' (Is 10/10), וּמַצֻּהֲרַיִם יָקֻם

חֶלֶד, '<your> life will be (brighter) than noontime'
(Jb 11/17);   cf. Ps 4/8.

581 (b) Pronouns are frequently omitted when clear from the
     context:

582 (i) When subject of an infinitive, e.g. בַּהֲפֹךְ אֶת־הֶעָרִים
     (Gn 19/29), וַיְהִי כִּשְׁמֹעַ אֶת־הַדָּבָר הַזֶּה (I Kg 20/12), es-
     pecially when this is indefinite, e.g. כְּשַׁסַּע הַגְּדִי
     (Ju 14/6), כְּבַשֵּׁל הַבָּשָׂר (I Sm 2/13).

583 (ii) When subject of a participle, e.g. וְהִנֵּה עֹמֵד (Gn
     24/30), וְגַם הֹלֵךְ לִקְרָאתְךָ (Gn 32/7);   cf. Gn 37/15, Am
     7/1, Jo 8/6. Note especially, in an indefinite con-
     text, וּלְבֵנִים אֹמְרִים לָנוּ עֲשׂוּ (Ex 5/16).

584 (iii) When object of a verb, e.g. וַיָּבֵא אֶל־הָאָדָם (Gn
     2/19), וַתָּשֶׂם אֶל־הַמִּטָּה (I Sm 19/13);   cf. I Sm 17/35,
     Gn 18/7, II Kg 4/5.

585 (c) Brachylogy, i.e. when the common object of a verb
     is omitted, e.g. נָשָׂא (קוֹל) (Is 3/7, 42/2), כָּרַת (בְּרִית),
     (I Sm 20/16, II Ch 7/18), הִפִּיל (גּוֹרָל) (I Sm 14/42, Jb
     6/27), שִׂים (לֵב) (Jb 4/20, Is 41/20), הֵשִׁיב (דָּבָר) (Jb
     13/22).

586 (d) After numerals, when clear from the context, certain
     expressions are omitted, e.g. שֶׁקֶל (II Sm 18/12, Nu
     7/68), אִישׁ (II Sm 8/13), יוֹם (II Kg 25/1), אֵפָה (Ru
     3/15, 17).

587 (e) A verb may be omitted when clear from the context,

e.g. אָבִי יִסַּר אֶתְכֶם בַּשּׁוֹטִים וַאֲנִי בָּעַקְרַבִּים (II Ch 10/11,
14;   contrast I Kg 12/11, 14!);   cf. Jo 24/15.   This
often occurs with the particle פֶּן (cf. § 461).

588   (f) Omissions frequently occur with negatives:

589   (i) אַיִן (cf. § 409), e.g. הֲיֵשׁ י' בְּקִרְבֵּנוּ אִם־אָיִן (Ex
        17/7).

590   (ii) לֹא (cf. § 398), e.g. וַיֹּאמֶר לֹא כִּי צָחָקְתְּ (Gn 18/15).

591   (iii) אַל (cf. § 403), e.g. אַל בְּנֹתַי (Ru 1/13).

592   (g) The oath formula is often omitted, e.g. אִם־יִרְאֶה אִישׁ
        בָּאֲנָשִׁים הָאֵלֶּה . . . אֵת הָאָרֶץ הַטּוֹבָה (Dt 1/35);   cf. Gn
        31/52.

593   (h) Aposiopesis, i.e. when the conclusion of a statement,
        such as the apodosis of a condition is omitted, e.g.
        אִם־תִּשָּׂא חַטָּאתָם וְאִם אַיִן מְחֵנִי נָא (Ex 32/32);   cf. I Sm
        12/14, Gn 50/15, Nu 5/20, II Ch 2/2.

594   (i) Sometimes a single word may constitute an elliptical
        utterance, e.g. וַיֹּאמֶר עֵד (I Sm 12/5), וַתֹּאמֶר שָׁלוֹם (II
        Kg 4/23, 26), לָשֶּׁלַל (II Kg 3/23).

BIBLIOGRAPHY

Albrecht, C. "Die Wortstellung im hebräischen Nominalsatze,"
  Zeitschrift für die alttestamentliche Wissenschaft, 7
  (1887), 218-24; 8 (1888), 249-63.

Brockelmann, C. Hebräische Syntax. Neukirchen, 1956.

Davidson, A. B. Hebrew Syntax. 3rd ed. Edinburgh, 1901.

Donner, H. and Röllig, W. Kanaanäische und aramäische In-
  schriften. 3 vols. Wiesbaden, 1962-4.

Driver, G. R. "Gender in Hebrew Numerals," Journal of Jewish
  Studies, 1 (1948), 90-104.

Driver, S. R. A Treatise on the Use of the Tenses in Hebrew.
  3rd ed. Oxford, 1892.

Goetze, A. "The So-Called Intensive of the Semitic Languages,"
  Journal of the American Oriental Society, 62 (1942), 1-8.

Gordis, R. "The Asseverative Kaph in Ugaritic and Hebrew,"
  Journal of the American Oriental Society, 63 (1943), 176-8.

Gordon, C. H. Ugaritic Textbook [Analecta Orientalia, 38].
  Rome, 1965.

Meek, T. J. "Again the Accusative of Time in Amos 1:1,"
  Journal of the American Oriental Society, 61 (1941), 190-1.

Meek, T. J. "The Co-ordinate Adverbial Clause in Hebrew,"
  American Journal of Semitic Languages, 47 (1930/1), 51-2.

Meek, T. J. "The Hebrew Accusative of Time and Place," Journal of the American Oriental Society, 60 (1940), 224-33.

Meek, T. J. "Result and Purpose Clauses in Hebrew," Jewish

Quarterly Review, 46 (1955/6), 40-3.

Meek, T. J. "The Syntax of the Sentence in Hebrew," Journal
of Biblical Literature, 64 (1945), 1-13.

Nötscher, F. "Zum emphatischen Lamed," Vetus Testamentum, 3
(1953), 372-80

Pope, M. H. "'Pleonastic' Wāw before Nouns in Ugaritic and
Hebrew," Journal of the American Oriental Society, 73
(1953), 95-8.

Rubinstein, A. "A Finite Verb continued by an Infinitive Absolute in Biblical Hebrew," Vetus Testamentum, 2 (1952), 362-7.

Schlesinger, K. "Zur Wortfolge im hebräischen Verbalsatz,"
Vetus Testamentum, 3 (1953), 381-90.

Scott, R. B. Y. "Secondary Meanings of אַחַר, After, Behind,"
Journal of Theological Studies, 50 (1949), 178-9.

Speiser, E. A. "Pitfalls of Polarity," Language, 14 (1938),
187-202.

Thomas, D. W. "A Consideration of Some Unusual Ways of Expressing the Superlative in Hebrew," Vetus Testamentum, 3
(1953), 209-24.

Weingreen, J. "The Construct-Genitive Relation in Hebrew
Syntax," Vetus Testamentum, 4 (1954), 50-9.

Wernberg-Møller, P. "Observations on the Hebrew Participle,"
Zeitschrift für die alttestamentliche Wissenschaft, 71
(1959/60), 54-67.

Wernberg-Møller, P. "'Pleonastic' Waw in Classical Hebrew,"
Journal of Semitic Studies, 3 (1958), 321-6.

Wevers, J. W. "Semitic Bound Structures," Canadian Journal
of Linguistics, 7 (1961), 9-14.

TABLE OF REFERENCES

Gn	1/1	162, 475, 489	Gn	3/1	385, 487	Gn	4/10	124
	1/2	72, 494		3/3	175, 461		4/13	577
	1/4	58, 475		3/4	205		4/15	523
	1/5	273, 430, 574		3/5	109, 213, 440		4/26	177
	1/10	273, 451		3/6	378, 577		5/20	97
	1/11	274		3/10	573		6/1	445
	1/14	228, 278		3/11	120, 423		6/2	326
	1/16	277		3/12	572		6/4	360, 576
	1/20	286		3/13	32, 118, 572		6/5	75, 391, 490, 562
	1/22	475		3/14	56, 173, 444		6/8	432, 572
	1/27	50, 571		3/16	438		6/12 f.	444
	2/4	109, 241		3/19	311, 574, 577		6/13	343, 376, 532
	2/5	408		4/1	345		6/15	486
	2/7	53, 322		4/2	70, 561, 572		6/17	68, 214
	2/8	571		4/3	324		6/18	111, 298
	2/9	105		4/4	378, 434		6/21	168
	2/15	110		4/5	395, 574		7/1	57, 372
	2/16	170		4/7	106, 514, 578		7/9	100
	2/17	194, 205, 396, 431, 574		4/8	70, 303		7/11	99
	2/18	192, 399		4/9	163, 577		7/13	95
	2/19	584					7/15	100
	2/23	87, 273					7/19	178, 349
							7/21	250
							7/22	326

Gn			Gn			Gn		
8/3	206		13/10	371		18/10	262	
8/5	206		13/12	310, 572		18/13	385	
8/7	92		13/14	360		18/14	262, 318	
8/21	395, 576		13/15	573		18/15	398, 590	
8/22	431		13/16	465		18/18	179, 494	
9/4	248, 388, 558		13/17	274		18/22	370	
9/6	245		14/10	16		18/24	365,477	
9/10	326		14/17	505		18/25	256	
9/11	320		14/18	572		18/26	440, 453	
9/24	77		14/19	29, 82		18/27	527	
9/25	80		14/22	164		18/28	96, 247	
9/28	360		15/1	360, 402		18/32	388	
10/2	430		15/5	62		19/1	219	
11/3	132, 191		15/11	287		19/4	167, 313, 327, 508	
11/4	494		15/12	196, 227		19/8	253, 559	
11/7	132, 191		15/13	539		19/15	262, 499	
11/9	160		15/15	252		19/17	295	
11/31	309		15/18	42		19/29	582	
12/1	238, 272		16/3	70		19/32	191	
12/2	278		16/5	110		19/33	74	
12/4	97		16/11	300		19/34	323	
12/7	90, 218		16/12	242		20/3	214, 291	
12/8	323		17/5	59, 550		20/4	379	
12/13	175, 367, 520		17/10	209		20/6	193	
12/14	58, 262, 504		17/15	447, 553		20/9	172	
			17/18	460, 547		20/10	526	
13/6	571		17/21	268		20/17	300	
13/8	561, 577		18/3	510, 514		21/5	59	
			18/7	178, 584		21/8	59	
			18/7 f.	83		21/14	287	

Gn	21/16	184, 204, 272, 401	Gn	25/6	498	Gn	29/17	562
				25/11	329		29/19	317
	21/22	484		26/8	496		29/27	59
	21/23	72		26/11	218		30/8	335
	21/30	521		26/24	56		30/16	74
	22/6	85		26/27	494		30/31	225
	22/7	277		26/28	335		30/34	460, 547
	22/8	572		26/29	331, 332, 391		30/36	40, 73
	22/12	451					31/8	453
	22/13	352		26/33	273, 311		31/13	82
	22/14	492		27/3	54		31/14	230
	22/16	363, 533		27/4	175, 187, 517, 521		31/15	206, 280
	22/18	533					31/20	291, 418, 489
	24/4	70, 179		27/6	572			
	24/6	461		27/10	521		31/21	88
	24/8	74, 390		27/15	73, 340		31/25	572
	24/12	70, 331		27/21	118		31/27	226
	24/18	224		27/29	104		31/32	162, 330
	24/19	457, 495		27/33	380, 508		31/38	118
	24/22	499		27/34	107, 378		31/43	573
	24/25	330		27/36	118		31/52	561, 577, 592
	24/30	583		27/42	59, 475			
	24/35	269		27/45	507		32/7	583
	24/42	479		27/46	514		32/9	94
	24/51	564		28/5	29		32/10	331
	24/54	328		28/9	292		32/12	461
	24/56	494		28/15	457		32/19	440
	24/58	171, 540		28/17	127		32/23	74
	24/65	86, 577		28/20	514		32/27	554
	25/1	224		29/7	194		32/29	447

Gn	32/31	299	Gn	40/5	131	Gn	44/3 f.	235
	34/7	172		40/14	347		44/4	55
	34/12	256		40/16	384		44/7	256
	34/13	468		41/1	68		44/15	256, 571
	34/30	48		41/8	23		44/16	125, 378
	35/5	81		41/19	273		44/20	478
	36/7	76, 318		41/27	234		44/22	511
	36/10	114, 561		41/32	289		44/28	205, 389
	37/2	571		41/35	350		45/4	463
	37/11	572		41/38	256		45/28	508
	37/15	167, 583		41/40	57, 390		46/4	379
	37/16	213		41/43	210		47/6	115
	37/17	358		41/46	503		47/18	56, 98
	37/21	57		41/49	311		48/7	288
	37/22	367, 519		42/16	449		48/19	551
	37/26	124		42/18	190		49/7	180
	37/29	407		42/25	9		49/25	285, 348
	37/32	543		42/28	118		50/15	593
	38/7	562		42/35	9		50/19	540
	38/24	316		42/37	170	Ex	1/12	264
	39/5	228		43/3	422, 555		2/6	71
	39/6	46		43/4	479		2/18	226
	39/7	299		43/7	167		2/23	74, 319
	39/9	247, 533		43/10	118, 166,		3/1	359
	39/10	15, 258,			449, 515		3/5	463, 537
		531		43/16	62		3/7	376
	39/20	489		43/17	62		3/12	452
	39/23	247, 407,		43/25	167		3/13	512, 577
		533		43/27	67		4/1	167
	40/3	489		43/32	168		4/9	379

Ex	4/10	399	Ex	14/28	314	Ex	21/29	232
	5/3	243		15/1	177		21/31	443
	5/10	407		15/12	177		21/32	443
	5/16	583		15/13	129		22/8	289
	5/19	195		15/14 f.	177		22/9	494
	6/1	167		15/16	129		22/19	422
	6/3	249		16/3	243, 546		23/30	16
	7/15	278		16/18	491, 575		24/4	349
	7/19	42		16/27	324		24/8	290
	7/20	244		17/7	291, 409,		29/37	47
	9/16	521, 551			589		29/38	486
	9/18	82		18/4	249, 563		30/7	100
	9/25	313, 327		18/17	399, 562		31/14	104
	9/27	33		18/20	539		31/16	195
	10/9	248		18/22	338		32/1	191
	10/17	390		19/11	268		32/9	46
	12/3	131		19/18	376, 533		32/12	252
	12/8	293		19/19	221		32/13	130
	12/11	494		20/4	348		32/26	121
	12/16	280		20/10	433		32/30	356
	12/19	250		20/12	286		32/32	593
	12/37	257		20/13-17	173		33/16	534
	12/48	209		20/20	175, 424,		34/2	268
	12/51	290			521, 523		34/6	72
	13/2	250		20/26	287, 466		34/10	25
	13/7	56, 475		21/2	278		35/22	293
	13/10	63		21/4	232		37/10	43
	14/11	394		21/12	173, 205		39/17	68
	14/15	125		21/16	433		40/37	514
	14/19	375		21/23	352	Lv	4/2	325

Nu	34/6	441	Dt	5/31	106	Dt	10/19	33
	35/23	400		6/3	38		10/21	341
	35/24	290		7/5	553		11/2-4	490
	36/2	245		7/6	491		11/10	35, 463
Dt	1/3	99		7/7	93, 319,		11/27	469, 514
	1/9	169			534		11/28	358, 469
	1/12	169		7/9	72, 266		11/30	54, 359
	1/16	132		7/12	72, 489		12/7	492
	1/30	341		7/24	491		12/11	35
	1/35	592		7/26	298		12/15	559
	1/44	168		8/1	108		12/20	184
	2/23	310		8/10	162		12/22	59, 491
	3/26	366		8/11	195		12/23	328
	4/21	109		8/16	82		13/4	479, 542
	4/24	215		8/19	73, 164		13/7	185
	4/25	198		9/7	186, 464		13/15	204, 485,
	4/32	256		9/8	275			561
	4/37	353		9/11	484		14/24	318
	4/40	175, 466,		9/16	491		15/2	209
		522		9/18	291		15/5	393
	4/41	177		9/20	199, 275		16/12	490
	4/42	420		9/21	274		16/20	16
	5/1	300		9/24	316		17/4	485
	5/3	107		9/25	56		17/14	184, 545
	5/8	273, 323		9/27	273		17/15	561
	5/9	270		9/28	420		20/1	82
	5/14	98		10/1	40		22/8	222, 315
	5/23	494		10/10	193		23/15	358
	5/29	74, 546		10/17	47		26/5	249
	5/30	272		10/18	29		27/6	53

Dt	28/23	286	Jo	5/13	282, 455	Ju	1/19	397
	28/55	418		7/7	547		1/24	215
	28/56	203		7/21	82		1/28	205
	28/61	399		7/25	53		2/11 f.	491
	28/62	249, 352		8/2	359		3/12	489, 533
	28/67	546		8/3	56		3/19	339
	29/17	461		8/6	583		3/26	311
	30/3	315		8/10	224		4/8	171
	30/6	365		8/13	323		4/9	427, 557
	32/7	101, 442		8/14	224		4/11	310
	32/10	177		8/22	116		4/14	114
	32/17	539		8/30	177		5/7	472
	33/11	321		8/33	82		5/10	30
Jo	1/7	491		9/16	360, 500		5/28	355
	1/15	263		9/24	59		6/14	74
	2/5	196, 204		10/7	315		6/17	472
	2/14	72		10/9	491		6/27	260
	2/15	84, 355		10/12	177		6/28	58, 218
	2/17	33, 74		10/24	91		6/31	311
	2/20	74		10/33	177		7/3	121
	3/7	466, 522		11/21	333		7/4	113
	3/14	29		14/11	256		7/5	92
	4/4	96		15/10	64		7/11	231
	4/6	469		15/13	307		7/12	129, 471,
	4/8	96		22/8	335			536
	4/20	96		22/17	59		7/14	422
	4/21	469, 514		23/1	489		7/19	210
	4/22	574		24/15	192, 587		8/6	228, 450
	4/23	468	Ju	1/1	92, 572		8/7	345
	5/2	571		1/12	463			

Ju	8/11	29, 82	Ju	20/20	277	I Sm	8/6	262
	8/19	166, 515		20/32	263		8/7	573
	9/17	295		21/21	234		8/19	553
	9/48	490		21/25	568		9/1	41
	9/51	355	I Sm	1/7	102, 254		9/2	76
	11/27	342		1/8	167		9/3	30
	11/40	63		1/9	207		9/4	409
	12/5	271, 398, 445		1/16	373		9/5	179, 235
				1/22	572		9/7	340
	12/6	308		1/23	184, 545		9/9	84, 92, 309
	12/8	322		1/28	381			
	12/14	96		2/2	422		9/11	57, 237
	13/8	572		2/3	225		9/12	266, 481
	13/21	207		2/7	384		9/14	236
	13/23	459, 515		2/11	213		9/15	162
	14/6	256, 582		2/13	582		9/16	262
	14/9	206		2/28	210		9/20	271, 273, 578
	14/16	391, 439		3/5 f.	225			
	14/18	317, 459		3/6	226		9/21	33
	15/2	185		3/8	226		9/22	257
	15/13	205		3/12	204		9/27	237
	15/14	235, 572		3/21	207		10/1	451
	16/15	527		4/19	306		10/3	95
	16/21	213		5/9	313, 327, 360, 500		10/11	118
	17/2	96, 340					10/12	439
	17/6	575		6/11	436		10/24	184
	18/3	120, 329		6/12	206		10/25	84
	18/12	359		7/5	356		11/7	81
	18/19	94, 543		7/9	356		11/12	541
	19/22	42		8/1	52		11/15	312

I Sm	12/2	161	I Sm	15/15	468, 532	I Sm	19/18	230
	12/3	573		15/20	178, 467		20/1	372
	12/5	594		15/22	238		20/3	261
	12/7	137, 341,		15/23	321, 440		20/6	136, 565
		344		15/26	321		20/13	59
	12/11	60		15/29	577		20/16	585
	12/14	593		15/35	306		20/26	421
	12/17	195, 562		16/4	541		20/27	378
	12/19	292		16/6	389		20/28	136
	12/23	73, 107		16/18	270		21/7	566
	13/5	335		16/23	86		21/9	568
	13/14	259		17/16	204		21/10	171
	13/15	73		17/26	8		21/16	288
	13/17	60		17/28	118		22/7	12
	13/17 f.	94		17/34	92		23/1	213
	14/9	351		17/35	584		23/3	387
	14/13	358		17/41	221		23/10	273
	14/15	81		17/46	229, 478		23/13	484
	14/16	270		17/55	456		23/15	64
	14/19	206, 311		18/4	313		23/18 f.	64
	14/30	387		18/8	388		23/20	284
	14/33	195		18/9	316		23/23	307
	14/34	304		18/10	254		24/11	490
	14/40	267		18/15	464, 490		24/12	379
	14/42	585		18/17	73, 242,		24/14	322
	14/44	449			388, 558		24/19	87, 475
	14/45	325, 336		18/23	117, 192		25/15	30, 489
	15/1	278		19/3	126, 511		25/19	70
	15/2	492		19/10	74		25/20	220,236
	15/12	226		19/13	584		25/22	311

I Sm	25/42	95, 436	II Sm	9/8	261	II Sm	586
	27/4	484		9/10	96	18/24	85
	28/7	42		10/3	521	18/25	206
	28/18	260, 533		11/11	456, 541	19/1	107, 546
	29/2	103, 281		11/25	59, 256	19/7	510, 515
	31/13	64		12/10	533	19/8	446, 514
II Sm	1/4	467		12/13	381	19/30	164
	1/9	30		12/14	557	20/1	128
	1/21	30, 419		12/30	436	20/15	64
	2/5	532		13/2	199, 275	21/3	189, 518
	2/6	72		13/5	367	21/4	410
	2/10	56		13/18	182	21/11	493
	2/23	351, 357		13/20	435	21/20	101
	3/11	319, 534		13/28	451	21/22	58
	3/17	564		14/4	34	22/34	579
	3/25	58		14/11	325	23/1	285
	3/30	273, 533		14/14	424, 523	23/15	546
	3/34	256, 399		14/20	521	23/17	246
	3/35	506		15/1	96	23/19	312
	4/1	234		15/4	122, 546	24/13	455
	4/2	95, 98		15/20	72	24/16	306
	4/11	387, 475		15/30	221	I Kg 1/2	65
	6/22	337		15/32	57	1/12	189
	7/9-13	182		15/34	323, 435	2/13	561
	7/28	115		17/5	107	2/15	322
	8/2	23		17/9	222	2/17	70
	8/13	586		17/16	273	2/18	295
	9/1	181, 426, 451, 487		17/22	311, 314	2/21	59
				18/11	294, 439	2/22	441
	9/3	426, 568		18/12	459, 515,	2/23	246

I Kg			I Kg			I Kg		
2/26	432		9/10	39		17/17	501	
2/27	198		9/26	339		17/24	118	
3/3	213, 390,		10/2	248, 337		18/5	324	
	559		10/6	67, 561		18/7	118	
3/7	193		10/7	305, 311		18/13	475, 493	
3/11	550		10/9	37		18/17	118	
3/12 f.	465		10/22	281		18/18	247, 534	
3/13	526		10/25	40		18/22	270	
3/19	468		10/29	246		18/23	160, 185	
3/24	83		11/1	438		18/24	229	
3/26	205		11/2	253		18/25	33	
4/7	294		11/3	234		18/27	172, 180	
4/12	64		11/9	91, 538		18/29	311	
5/5	274		11/39	366		18/32	52	
5/10	37		11/43	352		18/39	88, 115	
5/17	58		12/11	587		18/42	519	
5/25	168		12/14	587		19/3	302	
6/5	286		12/16	128		19/4	58	
7/12	73		12/31	14, 475		19/5	118	
7/14	65		13/20	308		19/6	224	
8/1	177		13/22	186		19/10	58	
8/9	392		13/23	360		19/11	399, 564	
8/17	337		14/10	361		19/12	399	
8/23	72		14/24	29		19/15	62	
8/25	393		14/28	509		19/19	99, 248	
8/27	387		15/13	573		20/12	582	
8/29 f.	299		15/20	13, 293		20/13	214	
8/31	469		15/23	57, 475		20/20	229	
8/63	571		16/10	99		20/21	182	
8/64	76, 318		17/13	388, 558		20/30	102	

I Kg	21/2	187, 352	II Kg	3/23	577, 594	II Kg 7/2	512
	21/5	219		3/26	228	7/3	125
	21/6	246, 452		4/1	94	7/7	302
	21/13	71, 524		4/2	478	7/9	213
	21/15	447		4/5	220, 584	7/17	162
	21/19	107		4/8	84	7/19	439
	21/20	363, 534		4/13	51, 196,	8/5	236, 475,
	21/21	361			480		490
	22/4	256		4/16	268	8/6	489
	22/13	28, 30		4/23	561, 594	8/7	494
	22/14	573		4/26	594	8/10	182
II Kg	1/2	542		4/29	446, 510	8/12	490
	1/3	394		4/43	125, 209	8/13	452
	1/4	574		5/1	372	9/22	311
	1/6	394		5/3	548	9/26	456
	1/13	74		5/7	271	9/32	346, 433
	1/16	394		5/8	477	9/37	169, 465
	2/9	181, 185		5/9	54, 270	10/3	93, 295
	2/10	226		5/10	189, 211	10/15	481
	2/12	220, 236		5/11	205	10/19	367
	3/4	68		5/13	387	11/5	576
	3/9	230		5/17	68	11/14	259
	3/13	403		5/20	449	13/2	358
	3/14	456, 459,		5/27	92, 266	13/11	491
		515		6/5	58	13/14	51
	3/16	16		6/11	129, 300,	13/17	207
	3/18	25, 228			301, 536	13/19	207
	3/20	475		6/26	89	14/8	177
	3/21	327		6/33	117, 125	14/26	426, 568
	3/22	92, 494		7/1	68	15/16	82

	II Kg			II Kg			Is	
II Kg	15/32	98	II Kg	23/17	29, 82	Is	13/3	380
	16/17	68		23/19	573		14/6	418, 421
	17/4	102		24/20	312		14/22	72
	17/6	42, 98		25/1	586		14/23	207
	17/18	392		25/15	16		14/31	211
	17/25	213, 251		25/19	29, 95		19/4	8
	17/26	260, 533	Is	1/4	162		19/8	30
	18/4	182		1/7	45		22/24	30
	18/10	98		1/15	382, 529		24/5	350
	18/14	294		1/17	203		24/10	105
	18/22	446		3/7	585		26/3	16
	18/30	59		3/16	533		28/4	30
	18/34	450		5/2	145		28/16	30
	19/3	408, 568		5/8	426		28/21	263
	19/4	8		5/11	30		30/19	205
	19/21	42, 361		5/12	177		32/10	418
	19/27	193		5/13	165		34/12	425
	19/28	534		5/14	420		36/15	59
	19/37	54		5/29	180		36/16	82, 190
	20/1	199, 571		6/2	4		36/18	461
	20/4	235		6/3	116, 132		37/28	193
	21/6	182		7/1	484		40/17	406
	22/8	573		7/2	9		40/20	539
	22/17	198, 353, 368, 533		8/6	274, 538		40/23	406
	22/18	90, 538		9/11	242		40/24	386, 413
	22/20	8		9/12	82		41/12	425
	23/4 f.	182		9/17	177		41/20	585
	23/8	61		10/4	555		42/2	585
	23/10	523		10/10	580		42/3	274
				10/15	256, 400		42/13	386

Jb 4/6 399, 435
 4/16 72
 4/17 169, 323
 4/19 373
 4/20 585
 5/2 273, 449
 5/7 437
 6/2 174, 205, 547
 6/8 546
 6/22 451
 6/25 202
 6/27 585
 7/6 426
 7/14 320
 7/18 281
 8/11 400, 420
 9/14 387
 9/15 156, 528
 9/18 203
 9/20 174
 9/26 334
 9/32 399
 9/35 337
 10/7 288, 530
 10/9 261
 10/13 337
 10/21 72
 11/17 580
 12/3 347

Jb 12/11 437
 13/12 283
 13/22 585
 14/3 385
 14/7 449
 14/13 546
 15/4 385
 15/16 387
 16/4 244
 16/10 244
 16/17 489, 530
 16/21 437
 18/19 72
 19/19 129, 535
 21/3 170
 21/7 380
 22/3 543
 23/3 546
 24/25 405
 25/5 314
 26/4 345
 27/3 30
 28/6 9
 28/14 399
 29/23 244
 31/1 428
 34/6 288
 34/17 385
 38/20 450
 40/8 385

Jb 40/10 72
 42/7 360
 42/11 131
Pr 1/29 533
 2/5 510
 3/18 104
 5/23 411
 6/13 244
 7/14 294
 8/21 476
 8/25 311
 8/26 9, 311
 10/10 244
 11/31 387, 513
 14/28 426
 15/20 168
 16/6 72
 17/12 212
 19/1 252
 21/16 207
 22/21 66
 23/7 414
 23/28 386
 24/11 458
 24/23 202, 414
 25/25 437
 30/10 151
 31/4 404
Ru 1/4 257
 1/8 234

Ru	1/12	446, 516	Ec	5/4	488	I Ch	4/5	95
	1/13	403, 591		6/6	515		4/27	312
	2/10	198		7/10	473		5/1	397
	2/21	378, 457		7/18	488		5/18	326
	3/12	567		9/12	262, 472		7/2	12
	3/13	56		10/3	472		7/5	13
	3/15	586	La	1/8	51		12/23	102
	3/17	586		2/17	492		15/2	397
	4/7	105	Es	1/19	296		15/19	68
Ca	1/1	47		3/13	210		21/13	75
	1/6	474		3/14	196		21/17	117
	2/7	128, 428		4/2	196, 410		22/4	411
	4/1	354		7/4	515		25/19	99
	4/3	354		9/1	210		26/13	442
	5/2	474	Da	1/4	29		26/28	91
	5/9	473		9/26	97		27/1	254
	6/7	354		11/15	14	II Ch	1/4	552
	8/4	128, 428		11/39	336		1/10	74
Ec	1/2	80	Ez	3/4	254		2/2	593
	1/9	471, 536		7/28	296		2/13	276
	1/13	182		8/25	91		2/16	362
	1/14	129		9/15	410		3/11	95
	2/12 f.	182		10/14	91, 442		6/22	469
	2/13	472		10/17	91, 538		7/18	585
	2/14	472	Ne	3/16-31	358		10/11	587
	2/16	472		5/15	96		10/14	587
	2/18	474		5/18	332		11/17	268
	2/19	543		7/2	261		13/5	284
	3/17	92		8/18	254		20/6	410
	4/2	210		9/32	59, 72		21/17	78

II Ch	25/5	14	Si	42/3	476	KAI	181/4-6	176
	25/9	480	KAI	4/1	129	UTB	51.i.39	81
	29/17	268		10/2	210		51.iv.34	205
	29/34	167		10/4	68		121.ii.10	205
	30/21	102, 254		26A 1/1	29		'nt II.iii.	
Si	10/7	323		26A 1/6	210		17-19	176
	25/21	476		26A 1/11	210			

References are to main discussions only.

אוֹ 443

אַחֲרֵי/אַחַר 357-362

אֵין 406-411

אַךְ 388-389

אַל 401-405

אֶל 297-308

אִם 453-458

אַף 383-387

אֶפֶס 425-427

אֲשֶׁר 462-469

אֵת (prep.) 338-347

בְּ 239-254

בַּל 412-416

בְּלִי 417-420

בִּלְתִּי 421-424

בַּעֲבוּר 521

בְּעַד 354-356

גַּם 378-382

וְ 430-442

יַעַן 363

כְּ 255-264

כִּי 444-452

לְ 265-284

לֹא 395-400

לוּ 459-460

לְמַעַן 364-368

לִפְנֵי 369-373

מָה 124-128, 428

מִי 120-123

מִן 315-327

מִפְּנֵי 374-376

עַד 309-314

עַל 285-296

עִם 328-337

פֶּן 461

רַק 390-393

שֶׁ/שֶׁ· 470-474

תַּחַת 348-353

122